Freeing Education

Steps towards real choice and diversity in schools

A collection of papers arising from the *European Colloquium on Education: New Educational Environments: Rights, Responsibilities and Initiatives,* held at the University of Oxford, Easter 1995. The Colloquium was organised by Human Scale Education and the European Forum for Freedom in Education.

Edited by Fiona Carnie, Mary Tasker and Martin Large

Hawthorn Press

Cover picture by Ivon Oates, using Logo from Human Scale Education with kind permission. Printed in Great Britain. Cover design by Patrick Roe, Glevum Graphics.

Printed in Great Britain by Redwood Books Limited, Trowbridge, Wiltshire

British Library Cataloguing in Publication Data

Freeing Education: Steps towards real choice and diversity in schools.-
Social Ecology Series
    1. Education, and state
    2. Steiner/Waldorf method of education
    3. Small, community, reluctant private schools
    I Carnie, Fiona II Large, Martin III Tasker, Mary
    379.2101

ISBN 1 869 890 825

Quotes

'In the United Kingdom. it is incompatible with libertarian position to return to either a pre-1965 selective system or to a pre-1979 comprehensive system. The most promising way of balancing individual rights and collective welfare is to retain an anti-selective comprehensive principle within a system characterised by unaccustomed and innovative diversity and choice.'
Professor David Hargreaves
Department of Education, University of Cambridge

'In many schools teaching is expected to follow syllabi that lay out what students will learn, as well as when and how they will learn it. But in a real classroom - whether school or the 'school of life' - there are living breathing people with personal needs and knowledge. The teachers' art is to connect, in real time, the living bodies of the students with the living body of the knowledge.'
Anita Roddick, O.B.E.,
founder and chief executive of The Body Shop

'The schools must be free to chart their own course, and it is parents and students - not the State- who have the primary role in holding the school accountable.'
John Chubb and Tenny Moe, Sunday Times, 9.2.92

'If a school system is going to meet everyone's needs then it has to start with the individual. It has to be designed from the bottom up. It has to allow the teacher the flexibility and authority to respond to the individual in the most appropriate way.'
Colin Hodgetts

'Genuine choice within a diverse system can only be made available if new schools are openly encouraged and publicly funded. Such policy also fosters the innovation and experimentation which is needed in education in order to identify ways forward for learning.'
Fiona Carnie

'Steiner education, with its emphasis on freedom from church and state, presents for the first time in the educational history of Ireland a truly free choice.'
Paddy McEvoy

'There is a good case to put for bringing 'traditional' values and alternative methodology into a mainstream education service which is desperately in need of fresh ideas. As more and more parents across a broad spectrum of faith and value systems come to understand this and seek to start their own schools, Muslims are realising that they are not, after all, alone in their quest for an education for their children which, in spirit as well as practice, ensures that 'pupils are to be educated in accordance with the wishes of their parents' (1944 Education Act, Section 76). To that could be added, "unless they are Muslims".'
Ibrahim Hewitt, Development Officer
Association of Muslim Schools

Parents have a prior right to choose the kind of education that shall be given to their children.
United Nations Organisation:
Universal Declaration of Human Rights (1948)

'Parents shall have the right to decide on the type of education and teaching to be given to their children of school age. Freedom of education and teaching shall include the right to establish a school and provide instruction. It is the parents' right to choose a school for their children until the latter can do so for themselves: it is the duty of the state to provide the necessary facilities for state or private schools.'
European Parliament: Resolution on Freedom of Education in the European Community (1984)

'There shall be freedom in education. Parents shall have the right to make provision for such education in accordance with their religious and philosophical convictions.'
European Parliament: Declaration of Fundamental Rights and Freedoms (1989)

Contents

Foreword: *Go for diversity!*

Michael Young

The authors in this book make out a marvellous case for alternative schools - a case which is all the stronger now that the government has become the schoolmaster or dominie of education, deciding in the most minute detail what children should be taught. It is an extraordinary change. Twenty years ago Britain had in an important sense the most libertarian education system in the world.

Almost everywhere else governments decided what and when and even how children should be taught. Children were treated as though they were interchangeable identities waiting to become data bases and governments would decide how to fill the data bases. Education was an instrument for making children as uniform as possible - identikit citizens who would be easily governable. Britain was the great exception. Individual teachers, admittedly with an eye to the cursed examination boards, could decide what to teach. But relative to other countries they were the kings and queens of their classrooms.

How different it is now! Teachers have lost their power. The bureaucrats have taken over. We have no curriculum for West Sussex, let alone for a particular village school, but a National Curriculum with a capital N. A government which claimed to be in favour of less government has in education added more to its power than at any time since 1888.

The deadening effect of uniformity is already showing itself, and the more it does, the more we need schools like those which have sprung up at Hartland and Goole and Oakhill and Brighton and other places. I can still rejoice when I remember visiting Hartland or, more recently, when I toured around a Koranic afternoon school in a prefab in Tower Hamlets. In both these very different schools the teachers had pride in what they were doing. Their faces seemed to be shining as they talked about their work. Teachers with shining faces have children with shining faces. They believed in what they were doing, not because they were the creatures of the National Curriculum Council. Diversity is life.

So what is to be done? The 1993 Education Act has so far been a complete sham. It opened a window and so far has prevented anyone climbing through it, or even looking through it with any intentness. But it need not be like that. Schools have just got to keep plugging away and testing out the politicians and trying to overcome the tiresome obstacles they will put in the way of reform. This is because politicians, and even more civil servants are ruled by precedent. Once there is a breakthrough, there will be a chance. To do anything new in England you still have to pretend it is not new.

I would put my money (if I had any) on a Muslim or Hindu school leading the way in a local authority where ethnic minorities are organised politically, like Leicester. Muslims could open the door to Christians and Christians to Buddhists, and Buddhists to non-religious but libertarian schools of the kind that once formed my own child's paradise at Dartington Hall. Those were the nostalgic days when teachers (at any rate my teachers) did not talk about curricula. They talked about children, and they were child-like themselves.

What else? I would ask the Danish Government to start some of their free schools in Britain. We belong to the same European Union. Likewise Dutch schools and Swedish and German and Italian. Open things up on a European scale. Encourage the Baccalaureate. Go not for growth, but for diversity.

October 1995

Introduction

Freeing Education: Developing a Third Sector Alliance

Mary Tasker

Has the revolution in British education that has taken place over the last fifteen years brought about greater freedom in education? Have parents gained freedom of choice under the neo-market system that has developed since the Education Reform Act of 1988? Or has the influence of the state in controlling what children learn and how increased to such a degree that choice and diversity have become a chimera? This collection of papers given at the European Forum for Freedom in Education Colloquium held at Oxford in April 1995 will attempt to answer these questions. It will also suggest some new directions that policy makers, parents and members of the community might find useful in working towards greater freedom in education.

The Colloquium was organised by the *European Forum for Freedom in Education* and by *Human Scale Education*. These two organisations are dedicated to freedom in education - freedom for parents and students to choose the type of schooling best suited to their needs; freedom from state control and bureaucratic constraint; freedom to found new schools and to develop innovative ways of teaching and learning. The European Forum was set up in 1990 in order to advance the cause of freedom and diversity in education which it sees as a basic human right. The 1948 United Nations Universal Declaration of Human Rights states that, **'Parents have a prior right to choose the kind of education that shall be given to their children'** and the European Forum sees its role as both extending and preserving this right. Initially the Forum's main support came from the countries of Eastern Europe which had only recently gained

political freedom - it now includes most of the European countries
and at Oxford a record 250 participants came from 31 countries
ranging from Ireland to Armenia. Some of the newest and smallest
of the European countries were represented - for example Estonia
and Croatia, Latvia and Slovenia.

Human Scale Education was founded in 1987 with the aim of
putting into practice the ideas of E.F.Schumacher, author of *Small
is Beautiful,* as they apply to education. It is HSE's belief that
smallness of scale helps to create the interpersonal relationships
that enable children and young people to become confident and
resourceful individuals, capable of respecting and caring for each
other and for the environment. HSE works with parents and local
groups to help start up small community schools, preserve existing
ones where possible and to encourage large schools to break down
into smaller units on the same site - the principle of minischooling.
It has from the start campaigned for the public funding of small,
parent-run schools - schools that are non-selective and non-
feepaying - sharing with the European Forum the conviction that
parental choice of education is a basic human right. Both HSE and
the Forum see educational pluralism and diversity as fundamental
to a free and democratic society.

At the Oxford Colloquium members of the Forum and HSE
came together to explore ways of bringing about more variety and
freedom of choice in the educational systems of their respective
countries. Some European countries have traditionally maintained
a wide variety of schools in both private and public sectors and we
have much to learn from their experience. In Denmark, for
example, 20% of all schools are 'private' schools attended by 10%
of the school age population. These schools have been established
in response to parental demand and they are funded by the state
to the tune of 85% of their running costs and, where a new school
is to be founded, almost all of the capital costs. Within this
category of state funded private schools are included Rudolf
Steiner schools, progressive free schools and Muslim schools. In
Holland 75% of all schools are 'private' - mostly Protestant or
Roman Catholic schools but also small schools, Steiner schools,
Montessori Schools, Freinet Schools, Jena Plan Schools, Dalton
Plan Schools. All are funded on an equal basis. These countries see
the existence of a diverse and flourishing private sector as an

expression of political pluralism appropriate to a democratic society. In the United Kingdom we too have a flourishing private sector - the 'public' schools. These are in fact private schools not funded by the state and free of state interference. They are not, for example, required to follow the National Curriculum. Many of these schools are boarding schools charging high fees - at the most prestigious schools these range from £10,000 to £12,000 per annum. The existence of the public schools could be seen as indicative of a healthy degree of choice and diversity in our society and many of them are outstanding in their academic and sporting achievements. But it is precisely because these schools are not state funded and charge fees, therefore catering by and large for the children of the wealthy, that they cannot be seen as democratic but rather as socially divisive. Freedom of choice in the U.K. is for the rich and relatively well off.

Many parents who do not fall into these financial brackets are also keen to exercise their right to choose and it is to this 'consumer' demand that the Government has responded with its policy of choice and diversity. Parents can indeed 'choose' from a range of state supported schools - from Grant Maintained schools which have 'opted out' of local authority control, from LEA controlled comprehensive schools, some of which might be voluntary aided Anglican or Roman Catholic schools, and from industry sponsored City Technology Colleges. But all these different kinds of schools are following a uniform curriculum and mode of assessment. As Richard Pring points out in his paper *The Role of the State in Education* what the Government has created, under the mantle of choice and diversity, is a 'diversity of producers' aiming at a standardised product. (His use of commercial jargon is intentional). Parents who depend upon government support for the education of their children have to accept the government's view of what that education should consist of. As the experience of some of the authors in this book shows, there is little room in this governmental view for any alternative forms of education.

The complexities of the UK situation are discussed in detail by David Hargreaves in his paper *'Diversity, Choice and Excellence: Beyond the Comprehensive School'*. In his opinion both the main political parties are looking back to some golden age in education:

the Tory right to the days of the selective grammar school in the
years 1944 - 1965 and the Labour left to the model of the large
comprehensive school which prevailed between 1965 - 1979.
Neither is appropriate to the mid-1990s and the 21st Century.
What is needed is a diversity of schooling that is responsive to
parental wishes with - and this is a crucial proviso - enough state
intervention to ensure that the most vulnerable in society do not
suffer. He believes that parents who are dissatisfied with the state
system should be able to choose from a range of schools - schools
providing a specialist curriculum in, for example, science and
technology or languages or the arts, schools with particular
religious affiliations or with particular educational philosophies
and/or teaching and learning styles. These choices should be
offered to British parents as they are to Dutch or Danish parents.

In the United Kingdom small schools, minority religious
schools, experimental progressive schools - have so far been denied
state funding and survive precariously on a combination of charity
money, minimal fees, payment in kind and community support.
Many of them want to 'opt in' to the state sector but cannot do so;
as a consequence they have become known collectively as the
'reluctant private sector'.

Prominent amongst these schools is the Oak Hill School whose
attempt to 'opt in' to the state sector is documented here by Ruth
Deakin.   Oak Hill School in North Bristol is a Christian
evangelical school founded in 1984 and financed by parents and
the local community. It is one of over 90 Christian schools
founded in the last 15 years and is the first to try to take advantage
of the terms of the 1993 Education Act, flagship of the
Government's policy of parental choice. The Act states that
voluntary bodies - churches, parents, community groups,
businesses - that want to start up a new school and 'opt in' as a
Grant Maintained School have first of all to find 15% of the capital
costs incurred. If the Secretary of State accepts the application -
and so far she has not -then the school is funded on the same basis
as other GMS schools. So far applications have been turned down
on the grounds of surplus spare places in schools in the same area.
There is, of course, a paradox contained in the Government's
policy on choice and diversity: *without spare places you cannot have
choice but with spare places you cannot start a new school.* Ruth
Deakin has found herself in this double bind situation, so too has

Ibrahim Hewitt who writes here on behalf of Muslim schools. But the 1993 Education Act is on the statute book and once the invisible barrier is broken through and a school from the reluctant private sector is given state funding then the Act could become the launch pad for dramatic change.

Some of the radical reforms that are under way in the United States could provide models for change in the UK. Robert Peterkin, formerly a leading educational administrator in Cambridge, Massachusetts and Milwaukee, two cities well known for educational innovation, shows how school choice can lead to diversity of provision which can in turn transform education in the inner city. In Milwaukee the public school system is flexible and involves parents and teachers in the decision making process. For example, parents, teachers and administrators have come together to design a system of magnet schools (specialist schools) and citizens' groups are empowered to set themes for new schools - these themes may be religious, philosophical, ethnic, pedagogical. As a result the first publicly funded Rudolf Steiner school has been opened, as has the first school for African American boys and the first school to be based on the pedagogical ideas of Howard Gardner. The Milwaukee system also has a pilot programme for school vouchers to benefit low-income students who want to attend private, that is, fee-paying, 'alternative' schools that are outside the public school sector.

Another reform increasingly popular with the American public is the charter school movement. Charter schools are public schools (schools for the general public unlike 'public schools' in the UK) and are state funded but they are also autonomous in that they are run by the Principal and parent-teacher committees without interference from the local school boards. They can depart from the standard public school curriculum if they so wish, a right denied to any state funded school in the United Kingdom. Parents and local groups can apply for charters to run a school - so too can businesses.

As more local school boards turn to big business in an effort to cope with the seemingly intractable problems of education in the inner-city so increasingly do the values of industry and commerce take hold in the nation's schools . Schools for profit are those which private companies operate on the invitation of the school board. In Baltimore a profit making company, Educational

Alternatives Inc., runs nine of the city's schools; after three years attendance rates are up but test scores are not. According to Peterkin the Edison Project is the most 'responsive' to the opportunities offered by the privatisation movement. It is the brain child of Chris Whittle, of Whittle Communications, a consumer orientated publishing company which has already sold news and advertising packages to public schools and is, therefore, well placed in the business of shaping values and attitudes amongst the young. By 1996 it hopes to have opened two hundred new 'schools for profit'. While these business run schools offer real educational benefits - small learning groups and interactive information technology - it is necessary to make a clear distinction between the values of corporate capitalism and the values of an educative community. Schools are not businesses and children are not products.

Peterkin claims that such a variety of experiment and innovation has brought a feeling of excitement and energy to inner city schools in America. By contrast the effect of the National Curriculum and its associated assessment procedures has been to stifle experiment in this country, and after seven years of Government reform in education an atmosphere of cynicism and resignation prevails amongst many teachers and members of the public. The State has become more controlling and more pervasive despite its much vaunted commitment to 'choice and diversity'. The Conservative Government has made parental choice the main selling point of its educational policies but as various local research studies have shown and as the experience of the reluctant private sector suggests, this is choice in name only. Britain is increasingly a pluralistic society yet clings to an anachronistically uniform system of schooling, framing a set of traditional values that bear little relation to the individualistic and rights conscious values prevalent today.

Nevertheless in the mid 1990's there are signs of change and of hope in the cultural and political shifts that are taking place in British society. At grass roots level there is a growing realisation that local communities need to act together to bring about, change. The moral and economic failure of the free market policies of the 1980s has brought about a swing back to the values of community, cooperation and responsibility. Schumacher argued for the rightness of small scale in all areas of social life and believed that local communities should take responsibility for the way they live. These sentiments expressed over twenty years ago are reiterated in the mid 1990s by the new breed of social entrepreneurs like Dick Atkinson, founder of St. Pauls Community Project in Balsall Heath, Birmingham. The Project runs a secondary school funded by charitable trusts, a nursery centre, farm, enterprise and community centre and acts as the focal point of the community. It has formed a neighbourhood forum which is regenerating the whole community by linking with all the other agencies, residents' and multi-faith religious associations in the area. Different kinds of initiatives are occurring in other parts of Britain. For example, in Stroud, Totnes and elsewhere, communities have set up local trading exchanges with their own currencies of value; in Bath, Bristol and many other towns and cities, food cooperatives have sprung up to meet the growing demand for organic food and throughout Britain there are burgeoning networks concerned, for example, with personal growth, complementary medicine, environmental protection. The small school network is one of these grass roots movements: its growth is another indication of community regeneration and is interdependent with it.

Shifts and realignments along the political spectrum can also help to prise open the educational system and provide opportunities for new initiatives. Within the Labour Party old certainties are dissolving as the commitment to the comprehensive school model slackens. So Grant Maintained Schools will remain under a Labour Government, to be renamed Foundation schools and will be funded by the Local Education Authority following the abolition of the Funding Agency for Schools quango. This greater flexibility on the part of Labour could be an encouraging sign for small schools wishing to 'opt in'. The Conservative Government's policy of introducing market forces into education by way of parental choice has rebounded on itself with unintended consequences. The 'opting in' clauses of the 1993 Education Act were framed in the hope that the 'new' schools would be selective grammar schools. But there is little evidence of any desire among parents and local communities to bring back the old selective system, nor has there been the anticipated flood of existing Local Authority schools wishing to 'opt out' and acquire Grant Maintained Status. The creative ferment is among the new small

schools - the so called reluctant private sector many of whom want
to take advantage of the 1993 Education Act.

Within this sector, which could form an educational third sector
representing a bridge between the state maintained and private
(fee paying) sectors of the education system, there are now over
ninety Christian evangelical schools founded since the early 1980s,
not all by any means wishing to 'opt in' since this would entail
observance of the National Curriculum. Other religious and
'ethnic' schools have emerged over this period - Muslim Schools
(whose case for state funding is argued in this book), Seventh Day
Adventist Schools, Buddhist Schools, Hindu Schools and schools
for disadvantaged African - Caribbean children in the inner city -
for example, the John Loughborough School in North London. All
these schools wish to educate children in particular ways according
to a particular set of beliefs and are denied a chance of doing so in
the state sector.

In addition to these schools there has been a less rapid growth of
small schools, most of them allied to Human Scale Education.
Two of these schools, the Small School in Hartland and Dame
Catherine's School in Ticknall, Derbyshire recently received
encouraging reports from OFSTED. The Inspectors remarked on
the liveliness of the students, the innovatory teaching and learning
methods and satisfactory academic standards, and the close and
supportive relationships that exist within both schools. These
schools enjoy parental support and both provide a good education,
however that term may be defined, yet both have had their
applications for public funding consistently rejected.

The parent and community groups that have tried to start up
small schools over the last fifteen years feel a profound
dissatisfaction with what the state has to offer them in its uniform
and paternalistic system of schooling. Comprehensive schools are
too large, too impersonal and too rigid in their curriculum and
organisation. There is a genuine need for alternative models of
schooling. David Hargreaves believes that it is essential over the
next few years to gather evidence about the effectiveness of
different types of school provision. He maintains that the days of
the large comprehensive school are over; in its place we need a
variegated landscape of small learning centres more responsive to
parental and community needs and wishes and catering for the
interests and talents of all our young people. One memorable

feature of the Oxford Colloquium was the confidence and energy with which a group of 16 - 18 year olds, mostly from schools that were outside the state sector, articulated their views on education. Their emphasis was on relationships with others, on self knowledge and personal development and on practical solutions to the world's problems. Can the present monolithic and formal structures of state schooling respond adequately to such concerns? The evidence would suggest that it cannot.

The late 1990s could see the opening up of a new era in education. The legal framework, set up by the 1993 Act, is in place and grassroots enthusiasm and expertise is growing. It is estimated that there are about 200 schools which could form a third sector and some of these are coming together in a Third Sector Alliance under the aegis of Human Scale Education. Colin Hodgetts explains how the Alliance could play a vital role in bringing together schools that wish to 'opt in' so that applications for Government funding are made from a united body and not as a single institution as was the case with the Oak Hill School. In this way greater pressure may be brought to bear on politicians who are largely unaware of the intensity of parental feeling. Through networking together greater knowledge and understanding - and ultimately trust - can be built up between the schools. On this basis it is more likely that a convincing case can be presented to both politicians and the public. Crucial to this case are the Alliance's criteria for membership. Those schools which are exclusive and seek to indoctrinate by means of curriculum and ethos are in no position to claim state funding and would not meet the criteria drawn up by the Alliance.

The Third Sector Alliance may prove to be the lever needed to prise open the carapace of an ossified education system. Our European neighbours, including those in Eastern Europe, have an open and flexible approach to schooling but we appear reluctant to learn from their experience. One purpose of this book is to inform readers in the United Kingdom of the variety of school provision in many parts of Europe and in particular of the Danish system of funding for small schools. Radical educational change is possible but it brings with it both the need for flexibility and compromise and the need to hold on to basic principles of freedom and justice. The American experience warns us that it is sometimes necessary to be wary of those bearing gifts - schools are not business enterprises. We hope that the information and ideas presented here will be of use to parents, schools, and community groups intending to lobby politicians at local and national levels as part of the process of freeing education for real diversity, innovation and choice.

Mary Tasker

Contributors

Fiona Carnie is National Coordinator of Human Scale Education. She is the UK Representative of the European Forum for Freedom in Education and also a Trustee of Bath Small School.

Ruth Deakin has been involved in Christian education for a number of years. She is the founder and head of Oakhill School, an independent Christian school in Bristol, and Director of the Christian Schools Campaigns. She is researching into diversity and self management in schools for a doctorate at Bristol University School of Education.

David Hargreaves is Professor of Education at the University of Cambridge. He was the Chief Inspector of the Inner London Education Authority from 1984-1988. His publications include *The Challenge for the Comprehensive School* and *The Mosaic of Learning*.

Ibrahim Hewitt is Development Officer for the Association of Muslim Schools. He worked at the Islamia Primary School in London from 1984-1989. He was Assistant Director to the Muslim Educational Trust until 1994.

Colin Hodgetts is Consultant to Human Scale Education. He was Headteacher at the Small School at Hartland in Devon for ten years until 1994. Colin trained as an anglican clergyman.

Rudolf Mees is a banker in Zeist in Holland and is a former director of the I.N.G. Bank. He was a member of the National Advisory Council for Education in Holland for 15 years.

Paddy McEvoy is the Chair of the Irish Steiner Schools Association. He is from Tipperary, Eire, and teaches Humanities in the Holywood Rudolf Steiner School, Co. Down. He served in six state schools in England, in both primary and secondary sectors, latterly spending fourteen years with the London Borough of Brent. He returned to Northern Ireland in 1988 where he lives with his wife Carol and their four sons.

Robert Peterkin is Director of the Urban Superintendents Programme at the School of Education, Harvard University. His entire career has been focused on urban education and he is one of the leading advocates in the United States for urban educational reform.

Richard Pring is Professor of Educational Studies at the University of Oxford. He is Editor of the British Journal of Educational Studies. His publications include Knowledge and Schooling, Personal and Social Education and The New Curriculum.

Andreas Suchantke is based at the Waldorf Institute in Witten in Germany and lectures on teacher training courses around the world. He is active in ecological field work and nature conservation and has written a number of books about education and ecology.

Mary Tasker is Chair of Human Scale Education. She is Visiting Fellow at the University of Bath where she taught in the Education Department for 15 years.

Gary Prosser has an MSc from Bristol University 1994 in Development Administration and Planning and has been Oak Hill School's Development Officer for the last two years.

Sir Crispin Tickell is Warden of Green College, University of Oxford. He was UK Representative to the UN from 1987 - 90. He is currently Chairman of the International Institute for Environment and Development. His publications include *Sustaining Earth* and *Monitoring the Environment.*

James Tooley is a research fellow at the Centre for Ethics and Social Policy at the University of Manchester.

Michael Young (Lord Young of Dartington) is the inventor and founder of the Open University and the Consumers' Association.

He is Director of the Institute of Community Studies. When the
Education Reform Bill was debated in the House of Lords, he
moved two amendments in connection with parental choice and
the need for greater diversity. He has written a number of books
including *The Rise of the Meritocracy*.

PART I

THE CASE FOR FREEING SCHOOLS

Role of the State in Education

Richard Pring

Summary of lecture given to the European Forum Conference in the Oxford Union, April 1995

A major theme of the Conference must be the balance between professional and parental freedom on the one hand and state control on the other. I wish to introduce this theme by focusing upon the changes in that balance in England and Wales over the last 50 years. The example is local. But the issues are universal. In pursuing this theme I make four points.

First, I refer to the minimum role of the state as that was reflected in the arrangements after 1944. Second, I refer to the economic and social changes which have challenged that role. Third, I refer to the changing partnership which has resulted from those challenges. Fourth, I identify the underlying philosophical issues.

1. Minimum Role of the State

The 1944 Education Act introduced secondary education to *all* young people in England and Wales. For the first time education was to be provided according to 'age, ability and aptitude', not according to wealth or social influence or academic excellence.

The ensuing system was a partnership between central government, the local education authorities, teachers and the churches.

Let us look at each of these in turn. The government's role was to ensure that there was a proper financial and legal framework for an education for all young people; it had no voice in what should

be taught (with the exception of religious education). The real
employers of the teachers and owners of the majority of the
schools were the local education authorities (LEAs); there were no
state schools, only 'maintained schools' within a state *system*.
Although the LEAs had responsibility for what went on in schools,
in practice this was devolved to the teachers the members of the
partnership which really controlled *what* was taught and *how* it was
taught. The fourth member of the partnership was the churches -
the Church of England and the Roman Catholic in particular -
since they owned so many of the schools. As 'voluntary aided' and
'voluntary controlled', the church schools retained a measure of
independence within the state system.

There are two features of the post 1944 arrangements which are
worth noting. First, there was little reference to parents or to the
local community in this partnership. Second, there was immense
power over the quality of learning devolved to the LEAs and to the
teachers. The government or the state did not control the
curriculum. There was an underlying belief that the teachers, by
reason of their experience and their training, were the experts not
only in how to teach but in what to teach. Interpreted in the most
favourable light, they were the custodians of an educational
tradition that should not be interfered in by the politicians.

Such a tradition was to be guarded from interference from
government by an independent inspectorate - Her Majesty's
Inspectorate - who for 100 years had provided a critique and a
defence of education, unconstrained by political demands or
requirements. Furthermore, central advisory councils,
representing teachers, LEAs, the community, were established to
which the government had to refer in the development of policy. A
friend of mine in North Oxford, Dr Marjorie Reeves, was
appointed to the Central Advisory Council in 1947; asking the
Permanent Secretary John Maud what the responsibility of
members of the Council were, Dr Reeves was told that it was to be
prepared to die at the first ditch as soon as government gets its
hands on education.

A system of balance and constraint - but a system in which the
dominant partners were the teachers and the LEAs.

2. *Changing Context*

There were three aspects of the context of education which caused government to challenge the partnership so conceived.

First, the late 1960s and the 1970s saw an increasing criticism of the standards in our schools. The 'Black Paper', first published in 1967, claimed poor standards in literacy and numeracy; they claimed, too, poor standards as a result, so it was claimed, of the pursuit of equality. And that has been a constant theme in the criticism of schools. Adverse comparisons were made with our economic competitors.

Second, there was a growing disillusion with the economic relevance of what was taught. It was not a matter simply of the less able lacking the basic skills of literacy and numeracy; it was also a matter of the more able lacking the appropriate attitudes towards industry and commerce. There needed to be a shift of attitude and the support for the more recently arrived virtues of 'enterprise' and 'entrepreneurship'.

Third, there was a consciousness of the alienation of so many young people. They increasingly demonstrated their disillusion with education through disruptive behaviour or indeed truancy.

The consequence of these criticisms - and *perceived* failures - was that government felt that it could no longer trust the educational profession to deliver the goods. Much more central control over the system - over what was taught, how it was taught, and where it was taught - was seen to be required.

3. *Changed Partnership*

The last 15 years, therefore, has seen a gradual shift of power, a change in the partnership, a greater role for government. The key legislation is the 1988 Education Reform Act, but that was preceded by other Acts of Parliament which ate away at existing arrangements.

First, there was a reform of governing bodies. Each school was to have a governing body which would represent the interests of parents, teachers and the local community (including, where possible, employers). Such governing bodies would be given much

greater responsibility for the running of the school - eventually the
management of resources and an overview of the curriculum.

Second, however, following the 1988 Education Reform Act, a
major shift in the balance between the different partners was
created. The government, through the Secretary of State for
Education, could determine in detail what the curriculum of all
young people from 5 to 16 should be - the attainment targets and
the programmes of study leading to those targets. This was as
much a 'reform act' as was the French revolution a 'reform' of the
French aristocracy. Rather was it a transformation of central
government responsibility, in contrast with the minimalist position
outlined in Section 1 above.

On the other hand, this central control of curriculum was
established at the same time as a decentralised system of 'delivery'
- the creation of 'consumer power' through greater 'choice and
diversity' of provision. Money was devolved from local authorities
to schools under 'local management' arrangements; new schools
were established sponsored by industry and commerce, viz., City
Technology Colleges; schools were encouraged to opt out of local
authority control and become 'grant maintained schools';
independent schools continued to receive public subsidy through
the Assisted Places Scheme.

Hence, that changed partnership had a different balance from
the one established following the 1944 Act. The gainers were the
state, which now could control the curriculum, and the parents,
who in theory at least could exercise their influence by selecting a
school from a greater diversity of them. The losers were quite
clearly, first, the local authorities, whose power was undermined by
greater parent power and government control, and, second, the
teachers, who had less influence over the values to be promoted in
schools and who had to be much more responsive to parents'
requirements.

4 Philosophy

Two aspects of a changing philosophy which I wish to draw
people's attention to are the underlying social philosophy and the
language through which education has come to be described and
evaluated.

(a) Social Philosophy

On the one hand, there is much greater central control over what should be learnt - and no one has been prepared to die at the first ditch. It is as though those parents who necessarily depend upon government support for the education of their children must accept the government's ideas of what that education should consist of. There is little room for alternative forms of education within the state system or for competing educational philosophies.

On the other hand, there is the self-evident appeal to individual choice - to the fact that the consumer (the parent) knows best - not the provider, that is, the teacher or the LEA. Hence, a constant emphasis upon consumer choice as opposed to provider control.

How is it possible to reconcile the centralisation of the curriculum - the control by government over the minutiae of learning - with the apparent emphasis upon choice?

Such a choice, to be effective, requires for the parent a variety of objects or places to choose from - in this case, if not the curriculum (which is 'national' and controlled by the Secretary of State) then the place and mode of 'delivery' of that curriculum.

Furthermore, there needs to be a standardised and objective way of labelling those things which are to be chosen from - so that the consumer can be well informed and rational. Hence, a national curriculum with nationally agreed attainment targets and national assessment. Thus, it might be argued, there have been created the ideal conditions for a consumer-led choice of educational provision - a diversity of producers aiming at the same standardised product with an open and objective labelling of that product. The state's job is twofold: to ensure the appropriate labelling of the product and to regulate the market competition for the support of the consumer.

(b) Language

Accompanying this changed partnership and changed social philosophy is a change in language. Teachers no longer 'teach'; they 'deliver (someone else's) curriculum. Learners become 'consumers' - with all the rights and powers that consumers have over what the 'providers' have to offer. Education is seen as a 'commodity' which has to be promoted and sold like any other.

What previously was seen as a transaction between teacher and
learner, the outcome of which could not be foreseen, is now the
transmission of something both predictable and desired by the
consumer. The complexity of knowledge, judgment,
understanding and appreciation is reduced to finite lists of
competencies. Standards to be achieved, so often implicit in
educational practice, become the 'performance indicators'
declared by the external assessors. Advisers, once there to support
the development of teaching, become the 'auditors' whose job it is
to state the success rate based on the performance indicators.

Contrast this with the language which compares education to the
'conversation which takes place between the generations of
mankind' in which the young are introduced to the 'voice of
poetry, or history, or Religious Education' - a conversation in
which outcomes cannot be clear but in which they are enabled to
think and to question and to argue. Part, of course, of that
conversation is that of those who wish to see education more
vocationalised - addressing itself to the wider consequences of
initiating young people into activities which we judge to be
educationally worthwhile.

5. Questions

(a)   We have seen within the last 50 years in Britain a radical
shift from minimalist state intervention to one where the state
exercises control over what children learn and how. The state
intervenes in setting the goals and in regulating the market. Is this
how one should see the role of the state? Have the politicians
insight into what is worth learning that parents, teachers and other
members of the community do not have?

(b)   One consequence of this has been the diminution of the
powers and authority of the LEAs and of the teachers. Should the
teachers, custodians of a distinctive educational tradition, exercise
authority over what should be taught, not over merely how it
should be taught?

(c)   What power, in such a centrally controlled but regionally administered system, should the teachers have in determining the ends as well as the means of education?

(d)   Where is the place for democratically and locally representative bodies (such as the LEAs) in determining both the amount and the distribution of limited resources for different educational ideas? How assure, in such a system, a responsiveness to the aspirations and values of parents and other elements (such as the employers) in the community?

(e)   Finally, where is the voice of the learner *children* in all this? Should they too have a 'say' in what is to be regarded as significant?

Diversity, Choice and Excellence: Beyond the Comprehensive School

David H Hargreaves

Overview

In recent times and in various countries there has been considerable pressure to raise educational standards and levels of student achievement. As a means to that end there has been a drive from the political right to greater diversity of school provision and an increase in parental choice of school. In theory, this market approach should be self-correcting and so allowed to run its course without state intervention. The political left, whilst sharing the aspiration to excellence in the school system, has been thrown into a defence of some of the *status quo ante* and so at times into an anti-libertarian position. It is argued that diversity and choice in the UK are defensible, drawing from both left and right libertarian positions. Though the two are not by any means always compatible, some combination is intellectually tenable and a possible basis for policy. In this modified libertarian approach, potentially acceptable to both left and right, diversity and choice are taken to be desirable unless and until (i) some convincing argument and evidence can be adduced that the costs greatly outweigh the benefits, and (ii) it can be shown that any costs incurred cannot be reduced or overcome by limited state intervention. If these conditions cannot be met, people will not be persuaded voluntarily to forgo diversity and choice or there can be no adequate justification for politicians to deny diversity and choice. It is argued that, from the libertarian point of view, diversity and choice need to be positively stimulated to sustain democracy in pluralist societies. However, diversity and choice cannot be left to market forces, but some state intervention is justified to protect the vulnerable from the unintended and inequitable side-effects of market forces. It is incompatible with a libertarian position to return to either a pre-1965 selective system or to a pre-1979 comprehensive system. The most promising way of balancing individual rights and collective welfare is to adhere to an anti-selective comprehensive principle within a school system characterised by unaccustomed and innovative diversity and choice.

In Britain, as in many countries, the major political parties believe that school students need to reach higher levels of achievement and that the education system and schools need to be reformed to improve the quality of schooling. Everybody strives for excellence: it is one of the educational watchwords of the left and the right (and so increasingly mere rhetoric). There is no real agreement on the means by which this shared end of excellence might be achieved. Indeed, the cross-party agreement on some aspects of recent reforms masks fundamental differences. For those on the political left, one component of liberty is freedom from exploitation by those with power and resources to secure educational advantage for their offspring, and so to reproduce inequalities in opportunity and a variety of inequities. For those on the political right, liberty includes freedom from interference by the State over the individual's right to educate in a way judged desirable by parents.

The political left in Britain is on the defensive, in part because the political right insists that choice is desirable, which indeed squares with a common-sense reaction to the notion. If it is a matter of choice or no choice, diversity or uniformity, people will favour choice and diversity, other things being equal. The political left therefore does not make a direct assault on choice and diversity, but rather on what are designated as their deleterious effects.

Whether there should be more diversity of educational provision and whether this improves educational quality and student achievement becomes partly a matter of debate on philosophical and political values and partly a matter of evidence about the effects, in terms of benefits and costs. Unfortunately, given the importance of the topic, the evidence in the US, UK and Australia is scanty (Braithwaite, 1992). In the absence of conclusive evidence, the discussion and debate is openly ideological and speculative, arguing what *might* be the effects if certain reforms were to be adopted.

It is the essence of a libertarian position that the state should not deny choice unless there are very powerful, reasonable and well documented grounds for so doing. Diversity and choice is the desirable state unless and until (i) some convincing argument and evidence can be adduced that the costs greatly outweigh the benefits, and (ii) it can be shown that costs cannot be reduced or overcome by limited state intervention. If these conditions cannot be met, people will not be persuaded voluntarily to forgo diversity and choice or there can be no adequate justification for politicians to deny diversity and choice.

This position is firmly grounded in a democratic conception of rights. In the UN universal declaration of human rights it is asserted that parents have a prior right to choose the kind of education that shall be given to their children; and other declarations of human rights adopt a similar line. This is not taken by most people in democratic societies to be highly controversial; the position is as attractive to the libertarian left as to the libertarian right. Most of the criticism of diversity and choice emanating from the left omits reference to declarations of human rights in the field of education as this is simply inconvenient.

Human rights in education are the source, in most European societies, of education, but not schooling, being compulsory. Parents are required by law to *educate* their children; that is an intervention by the state to protect the rights of the child. But to achieve this end by compelling parents to send the child to school would be an infringement of the rights of parents. From this basic position derives the freedom to create religious schools, since many parents want the kind of education that is based on and transmits religious values. In past times, religious schools meant different Christian denominations. In contemporary and more pluralistic Britain, the growth of religious but non-Christian schools, such as Islamic schools, is now testing the libertarian position of both left and right. For the right, Muslim schools pose a threat to Christian values and a common culture grounded in Christianity. For the left, Muslim schools promote racial segregation and undermine a multi-ethnic society.

The capacity for choice is not equally distributed in society. The greatest choice lies with better-off families who can effect choice above and beyond any permitted by a local education authority: either by moving house into the catchment area of a preferred school or by paying fees for a private school. Such choices by richer families increase the tendency of such schools towards socio-economic homogeneity of family background. There is evidence that increased choice will exacerbate this tendency: the schools in middle-class areas become more popular and those in working-class, inner-city areas less popular. As the popular schools become oversubscribed, schools have to choose the pupils rather than parents choosing the school, and the gate is open to some form of selection - by ability, social class or ethnicity.

'*Schools choose parents rather than parents choosing schools*' has become a campaign slogan of opponents of diversity and choice, seeing the right's talk of choice as a cloak for a return to selection by ability and thus a challenge to the principle of the non-selective comprehensive school. But are the criteria set above to justify the denial of diversity and choice met by the evidence? In relation to the first criterion, the costs of choice have not *as yet* been shown to outweigh the benefits. The evidence shows that choice exacerbates trends already in the system, namely for suburban, middle-class schools to be preferred to inner-city working-class schools. This is why middle-class families often choose their home on the basis of in which school's catchment area it stands. It can be argued by the right that increased choice benefits the relative poor and enhances equality of opportunity, since they do not need to move home to obtain their preferred school if the local school is disliked.

A contrary view is that those abandoning the less popular local school gain an advantage over those who remain there and that the less popular local school will become increasingly disadvantaged, for instance, in quality of teaching or outcome and perhaps enter a spiral of decline. Hard evidence on the precise extent of this shift in advantage and disadvantage precipitated by choice, as against what happens as a result of imbalances in social class and ethnicity relating to residential patterns in strict catchment areas without choice, is in short supply. It seems likely that where choice exists parents are less concerned about the location of their home, which has the desirable effect of increasing the social heterogeneity of inner-city districts.

Even in cities where choice of school is real and transport costs low, most parents choose the local school for the obvious convenience created by proximity to home and because the child is likely to have neighbourhood friends at the local school. Other things being equal, parents will choose their local school unless they have grounds for dissatisfaction with it - or a more distant school has positive attractions greater than those of the local school. This suggests that most parents want a local school that meets their preferences and their expectations of quality. Some parents will have preferences that cannot be met locally, such as a parent wanting a religious education for their child in a locality where the family religion is in a minority position. If many parents in an inner-city district make preferences against the local school, this is a strong indication of considerable dissatisfaction with the local school.

Under-subscribed schools have not, as predicted by the theorists of the right, withered away and by some kind of social darwinism been closed to the extent expected. On this matter, the political left is justified in expressing concern that schools which enter a spiral of decline might go through a very extended terminal phase to the serious disadvantage of their members. If some schools do, the state should intervene, and intervene quickly in the interests of students. If on examination or inspection the judgement is that the school is failing to meet adequate standards, then the school should be closed. Bad schools do not, as the political right has theorised, die of their own accord through market forces: bad schools may have to be murdered. The thesis that choice creates competition and competition drives up standards has yet to be proved. Even if it could be shown that it drives up standards on average, it seems likely that the average rise will mask a deterioration in some under-subscribed schools, which will tend to serve disadvantaged communities. On the other hand some under-subscribed schools do, somewhat to the dismay of the theorists of the left, recover and fight back, and more would probably do so if there were more active external support for them. There is now a range of school improvement strategies and those which are best applied to failing schools probably include a component directed to creating a stronger partnership between home and school. It is, then, very possible that the costs of choice can be reduced by appropriate intervention.

Among the over-subscribed schools, there is the possibility that they are selecting by ability, and there is undoubtedly some support for selection in the British Conservative party. Though schools can do so legitimately with the permission of the Secretary of State, most British schools are not so permitted, but some do so covertly and without embarrassment. Again, this should be prevented by stronger control over the criteria for admission to the school: inspection and enforcement of such criteria against selection on the grounds of general ability, social class or ethnicity is a justifiable state intervention to reduce the costs of diversity and choice.

Prevention is a better strategy than cure. All our schools are inspected once every four years. Inspection should as a priority focus on schools known to have academic outcomes well below national averages; whenever there is evidence of low parental satisfaction; and wherever schools are heavily under-subscribed (and therefore at risk) or heavily over-subscribed (which may mask selective practices). Preventive action and interventions might ameliorate the deleterious side-effects of diversity and choice. Until such interventions have been thoroughly tested, and further corrective action taken in the light of evaluation of intervention, it is not conclusively demonstrable that the costs of choice outweigh the benefits. The case against diversity and choice remains unproven in the UK and so denial of them is unwarranted.

Is there an alternative to a policy of persisting with diversity and choice and collecting evidence on the extent to which preventive and intervention measures ensure that benefits outweigh costs? The anti-libertarian alternative of the left in extreme form requires the abolition of private education and religious schools and requires every child to attend their local school. On this view the comprehensive principle requires there to be a local school which is attended by all living in the catchment area, with few exceptions (such as those in certain categories of special educational need). Every comprehensive school should have a similar student ability range, contain a social and ethnic mix, follow the same curriculum and offer the same opportunities. This, it is claimed, is the only way that a society can guarantee equality of opportunity to all its members irrespective of social background. Such an approach undermines freedom of choice in relation to education as well as freedom of assembly, and entails providing powers to officials to decide catchment areas or, when the catchment areas are not socially or racially heterogeneous and have an unbalanced ability range, to allocate (and bus) children to schools in order to attain some desired state of mix in relation to students' ability, sex, social class, ethnicity, religion etc. and if necessary in defiance of parental preference. That virtually no comprehensive school in practice has ever met this definition, whatever political party is in power, is ignored by the left.

This addiction to the mythical comprehensive school leads inexorably to the suppression of information. The ideology that the comprehensive principle means interchangeable schools within a uniform system means that any evidence against interchangeability threatens to undermine public confidence in the system. There is, and for many years has been, information on the variability between schools on a wide range of factors. The publication of such information by the political right, on the grounds that choice cannot be sensibly exercised in the absence of both diversity and detailed information about that diversity, has angered the political left for it undermines the ideology of interchangeability. It is true that some forms of 'league table' are misleading when no account is taken of school intake factors. It is disingenuous of the political right not to concede the point, and it is dishonest of some on the left not to admit that they are against the publication of even 'value-added' measures of difference in order to protect the myth of interchangeability against a public that is far from being duped.

There is no evidence that a restoration of the pre-1979 comprehensive system would be popular among parents; even among the political left in Britain it is currently in disfavour. Indeed, the fact the leader of the Labour Party has chosen to send his child to a grant-maintained religious school which is not his local school under local education authority control has caused dismay among many Labour Party supporters. It seems unlikely that an in-coming Labour government will adopt an anti-libertarian education policy.

The academic community on the political left is less libertarian. Two contributors to the National Commission on Education (Walford, 1992; Adler 1993) are broadly from the left and seek to restrict the infringement of individual liberty and choice in the interest of collective welfare and argue that a balance has to be sought between the two. At first sight these might resemble my own approach, but there is an important difference. The modified libertarian position I propose is one which approves choice in principle but permits intervention only when the effects of choice are demonstrably deleterious and costs can be shown irremediably to outweigh benefits. By contrast, some left positions, whilst not being overtly anti-libertarian by a thoroughgoing denial of diversity and choice, begin from assumptions that (i) choice is in principle dangerous rather than desirable, and (ii) enough is known about the effects of choice to justify the immediate introduction of restrictions on choice in the interests of a model of comprehensive education. Such schemes are, I believe, merely quasi-libertarian and in practice there is little to distinguish them from the fully blown anti-libertarian stance.

GeoffWalford (1992) accepts that there has never been a pure or full comprehensive system in the sense that all comprehensive schools are essentially equivalent or interchangeable; rather the comprehensive school masks selection according to the composition of the local community, which as noted above has been fully exploited by many middle-class parents. Indeed, he thinks this fact explains why there has been relatively little support for a return to an overtly selective system - it simply isn't necessary. He regards recent reforms from the political right designed to increase diversity and choice as replacing the iniquity of selection through catchment areas as selection by schools of those families with the greatest interest in education.

> The new forms of selection currently being put in place will mean that our society is likely to provide the poorest schooling for those children most in need and the best for children who already have the most advantages. This is not only a personal tragedy but is also a waste of individual and national talent.

Walford is predicting the negative effects of choice; before clear, hard evidence of them is to hand, and before examining whether such costs can be reduced by modest intervention, he believes it essential to devise some alternative. He seeks to reverse the trend to diversity, which he asserts entails inequalities, and favours the standard or uniform comprehensive model of old. The main problem, he asserts, is the selection process done by the over-subscribed school. To solve this problem, all parents are compelled to make several choices of school. If the school is under-subscribed, all parents who choose it get their choice. In the case of the over-subscribed schools, the only fair way to select students, he argues, is on a purely random basis. This means that the rights that many schools now give to families living nearby, or to those who have a sibling already in the school, would disappear. The only exception Walford allows is to students with physical disabilities who are given a right to attend their local school.

This approach would almost certainly mean that the more a school is over-subscribed, the lower the chance of local family getting a place. In the case of a highly over-subscribed school, it could mean that most of the local children would have to be transported to more distant schools. Walford recognises that this is not likely to be popular - the most obvious reason why local politicians would be disinclined to adopt it. In fact, the whole point of the approach is that it would be very unpopular.

> Random selection introduces uncertainty, and so it becomes necessary for concerned parents to work for high quality schools for all children rather than devoting their efforts entirely towards the schooling of their own children. Requiring all families to make a choice will broaden and deepen concern for education. More uncertainty in selection will ensure that high quality schooling for all children will become a political imperative.

Compel choice, in other words, so that as a result of the social engineering achieved through making allocation a lottery, choice will eventually become unimportant and not worth making. The scheme conveniently ignores the immediate short-term effects that would follow. If middle-class parents had their chances of getting a school of their choice substantially reduced, and were told their children would be bussed to unpopular schools with poor reputations, they would opt out of state-provided schools for private schools. It is difficult to see how this would raise the general quality of schools. Indeed, if raising the general level is the aim, there is more to commend the view that the middle classes need more confidence in the quality of their local schools and so to prefer them to private education. Walford's scheme would increase, not reduce, the private sector. However, it is unlikely that the Walford scheme will ever be put to the test: what prudent politician seeks to anger the electorate in the hope that they will in due course be thanked for their long-term perspicacity?

Michael Adler (1994) shares the view that comprehensive schools are far from being equivalent, but rather than, with Walford, seeking a means of making them so, he believes the attempt should be abandoned. Whilst all schools should have a common core curriculum, he advocates some curricular specialisation. Catchment areas are to be abandoned too. How, then, are students to be allocated to schools? Adler believes parents, students, teachers and counsellors should work together to decide which school is best suited to each child. This could be a helpful, if slow and costly procedure. That counsellors and teachers might well be inclined to give 'guidance in the interests of the smooth running of the system (all schools ending up with a reasonable intake) rather than the individual need (which could lead to some massively over- and under-subscribed schools) is played down. Acknowledging that over-subscription of schools would occur, Adler is forced to give allocative powers to officials who would implement

> a set of general policies, for example in relation to minimum, optimum and maximum school sizes and appropriate ability, social or racial mixes for schools.

In short, avoid giving explicit choices to parents, and instead devise a system of talking allocation over between families and professionals; if it doesn't work out according to what the politicians and the officials want the system to be like, let the officials decide. In short, for the scheme to work there may well need to be a resort to anti-libertarian measures by which bureaucrats know better than parents.

In the debate over diversity and choice the left argues strenuously for the collective good whereas the right appears to ignore the community and society. I want to argue that paradoxically the anti-libertarian or quasi-libertarian stance of the left is unlikely to move us towards the collective good whereas the diversity and choice advocated by the right might, within a modified libertarian approach, do so the more effectively in a modern pluralistic democracy.

The left's espousal of the comprehensive school assumes that in a multi-ethnic, multicultural, multi-lingual and multi-faith society, mixing the young of different races, religions, classes, faiths etc. in the common school is the best way to provide equity in relation to educational opportunity and create a tolerant society in which differences are respected for the benefit of all. Indeed it might. Where the local community is relatively homogenous in terms of race, religion and language, there is likely to be a commitment to the local comprehensive school which is perceived to be able to be responsive to local wants and needs and perhaps also be a focal point of community life. Even in communities which are relatively heterogeneous, there may be a strong sense of local loyalty and support for 'our' school. This is by no means incompatible with diversity and choice which has to allow the possibility - indeed likelihood - that almost everybody in a community freely chooses the local comprehensive secondary school designed to meet the needs of all.

But in other areas, parents may not want the standard, local comprehensive but may wish to choose from schools with different kinds of curricular specialisation (science and technology, the arts, languages); variations in educational philosophy or pedagogic preference; and of course religious affiliation. Particularly since the emergence of a national curriculum in the UK, such variations between schools do not entail the denial of a basic common curriculum between schools. The left often argues that such specialisations and variations damage national cohesion. But it is possible to argue that specialised schools enhance social cohesion within a sub-community (eg of a shared religion or culture) and in a pluralistic society there can be no national cohesion that fails to foster and build upon more local and specific forms of social cohesion. In a society that is highly homogeneous, the common school may contribute to both local and national solidarity. In a heterogeneous society, the common school may do neither. Diversity of schools may aid the cohesion of sub-communities. They do not, however, automatically generate national cohesion and could even damage it: national cohesion entails some form of civic education shared by all the variations and specialisations would be essential (Hargreaves, 1994). Some aspects of the debate on specialised schools do not easily divide into left and right views. I have heard ethnic minority groups on the left argue that Muslim schools are essential to maintain cultural, religious and linguistic identities; but some of the white, native British left think of such schools as imprisoning their children in their parents' cultural and religious frame. Social cohesion in a pluralistic society is perhaps best achieved by the avoidance of too little and too much diversity. It is a task of the contemporary British school, whether specialised or common, to transmit the recognition that British identity does not require the annulment of different values and loyalties (Dodd, 1995).

It is essential to gather evidence over the next few years about the relative effectiveness of different types of school provision. It is worth hypothesising - rather than assuming or asserting - that schools which become distinctive or specialised in some way are more likely to be effective and to promote excellence. At present the dominant version of the comprehensive principle entails an assumption that comprehensive schools, being essentially interchangeable in the interests of social equity and collective welfare, will tend to have the same aims, values and ethos. Equity, on this view, means uniformity of mission. In reality, some parents want a distinctive form of schooling and where it is provided they are more likely to be committed to its success. It is well known that parental commitment and involvement in schooling is a significant contributor to school effectiveness; diversity and choice may be one means of enhancing this important variable.

But it is not only parents whose commitment is enhanced by choice; the thesis can be applied to teachers too. On appointment many teachers know little about the kind of school they are joining, for in a system where comprehensive schools are supposed to be interchangeable, diversity of mission has to be under-played. Boards of governors and more particularly school principals do have distinctive missions nevertheless, but missions are difficult to achieve precisely because they are by no means always shared by the teaching staff. If schools were more diverse and open about their distinctiveness from the start, they would be more likely to recruit staff who share that mission and are committed to its realisation. Closing the gap between the most and least effective school, an essential element in promoting general excellence, is, I hypothesise, more likely to be achieved through shared missions within diverse provision than through attempts to restrict diversity and choice.

Some on the left seek to return to the *status quo ante,* that is the 1965 - 1979 version of the comprehensive principle in Britain, which is probably reaching the end of its useful life. There are those on the political right who want to use diversity and choice as a springboard to a revamp of 1944 - 1965 selection, which probably no longer commands popular assent. Both are retrospective and nostalgic: neither is libertarian. There is a way of providing for diversity and choice that retains a commitment both to the fundamental comprehensive principle of opposition to selection by ability and to a libertarian acceptance of some diversity and choice. This can be achieved neither through rigid state bureaucracies imposing uniformity of provision nor through self-correcting market forces: but modified libertarians have never believed in either and know that the good society is not built from such simplistic educational recipes.

Select Bibliography

M. Adler, *An alternative approach to parental choice* London: National Commission on Education, 1993.

R.J. Braithwaite, 'School choice as a means of attaining excellence in education' *Cambridge Journal of Education* 22(1)pp.43-54, 1992.

D. Bridges & T. H. McLaughlin (eds), *Education and the Market Place* London and Washington DC: The Falmer Press, 1994.

P. Dodd, *The Battle over Britain,* London: DEMOS, 1995.

T. Edwards and G. Whitty, 'Choice in English secondary education: lessons for America?' paper presented at AERA annual conference, New Orleans, 1994.

M. J. Halstead (ed), *Parental Choice and Education: policy, principles and practice.* London and Philadelphia: Kogan Page, 1994.

D. H. Hargreaves, *The Mosaic of Learning* London: DEMOS, 1994.

P. Munn (ed), *Parents and Schools: customer, managers or partners?* London
and New York: Routledge, 1993

T. Smith & M. Noble, *Education divides: poverty and schooling in the 1990s.*
London: Child Poverty Action Group, 1995.

G. Walford, *Selection for secondary schooling* London: National Commission
on Education, 1992.

Choice as a vehicle for the Revitalisation of America's Inner City Schools

Robert Peterkin

Today I hope to bring you some of the excitement and energy that school choice has brought to the American public, and in some cases, private schools, especially in my country's inner cities. Of particular emphasis will be the new charter school movement and the contracting initiatives which are bridging the gap between public and private education. I will also attempt to describe the renaissance of empowerment and pride displayed by local communities as they take advantage of new opportunities to redefine the educational process for their children.

Before I begin my examination of school choice and the charter/contracting phenomena, I will provide some background on the evolution of the school choice movement in the U.S. from my admittedly personal viewpoint. Any examination of the school choice movement must first start with review of the school reform movement. Modern school reform in the United States has recently completed an exhaustive, decade-long struggle for improvement in student achievement, especially for poor and minority students in the nation's inner-city schools; the movement was initiated in 1983 upon the release of *A Nation at Risk,* a report of the National Commission on Excellence in Education. The report, commissioned by U.S. Secretary of Education Terrel Bell at the behest of then President Ronald Reagan was as inflammatory in its rhetoric as it was alternately mundane and daring in its recommendations for improving the condition of education in the United States. I quote:

> ...The educational foundations of our society are presently being eroded by a rising tide of mediocrity that threatens our very future as a nation...

If an unfriendly foreign power had attempted to impose on America the mediocre educational performance that exists today, we might well have viewed it as an act of war.

Hidden among the recommendations was one to broaden the opportunity of parents to demand a wider range of programming in '...public, private and parochial schools and colleges...' which *they* deemed most appropriate for their children - in a call for innovation - *within and beyond* the public school sector.

From 1983 to the present, the school reform movement given birth by *A Nation At Risk* twisted itself through *at least* five iterations:

1. basic skill and graduation mandates imposed by governors and state legislators;
2. teacher reform initiatives which ranged from professionalization and empowerment to mandatory and voluntary (National Board of Professional Teaching Standards) competency testing;
3. national subject matter standards and assessments (National Goals Panel; National Assessment of Educational Progress);
4. decentralisation and school-based reform; and
5. 'theoretical' reforms (Gardner, Comer, Sizer).

The only common feature among them was the persistent presence of *school choice* as a partner, even when that partnership would seem antithetical, such as national standards *and* school choice. Choice in the U.S. is seen by some as an outgrowth of our noble experiment in democracy: freedom for the individual from the tyranny of the majority. As an African-American from the commonwealth that produced Horace Mann and the *common* school, the concept of freedom may seem more ideal than real. Nonetheless, the right to *choose* - products, residences, careers, churches and schools - is held up by school choice advocates as a fundamental right. With public schools, especially in our inner cities mired in mediocrity, celebrating their 'islands of success' but unable to produce *systems* of success, the right to choose the public or private school for one's child, and to have that choice supported by tax dollars seems eminently rational.

Let me take a few moments to explore the recent history of school choice. I am going to focus on the period from the late

1960's to the present, excluding religious and elite private schools and the post-desegregation 'freedom' and 'white-flight' schools in the American south. The issue of those schools in America is quite another matter, which I will address in the Q/A if you wish. My starting point is another period of dissatisfaction with school and governmental bureaucracies that exploded in America's cities during the late 1960's and early 70's. Citing cultural irrelevance, stagnant curricula and stifling bureaucracies, activists across the land established thousands of community-based schools; groups from the Black Panther Party to the sisters of the Sacred Heart of the Catholic Church opened private, non-profit, non-sectarian alternative schools.

Some of these schools worked with and for disaffected students who were 'turned off' by the 'regular' schools. Others were designed to reinforce the culture of their communities, largely communities of colour. Whatever the reason for their initiation, these schools were designed to meet the affective and cognitive needs of young people whose needs were *not* being met in traditional schools, and who *chose* the alternative schools over the traditional schools. I was the director of one such school, The Street Academy in Albany, New York.

By the mid-1970's, many of the community and alternative schools had closed due to financial pressures and a changing political climate. Their lessons of programmatic diversity and *choice* were not lost on the urban mostly-northern school systems, however, undergoing court-ordered desegregation. If disaffected students could be drawn to alternative schools for non-traditional curricula, pedagogy and thematic variation, could public schools 'magnetize' themselves to attract students from diverse racial and socio-economic backgrounds? After the violent opening rounds of the Boston Public Schools desegregation lawsuit and the subsequent 'calm' after magnet schools were introduced into the system, public schools across the nation hoped the answer was an emphatic 'Yes'.

In fact, magnet schools have proven to be a success with those parents, students and teachers who have been able to access them. Characterized by specific thematic foci, parental choice, heightened teacher expertise and selection, and additional programmatic resources, magnet schools have generated so much interest in their communities that *good* ones are frequently over-subscribed and school boards are increasingly asked to replicate the most popular themes in other schools in the district. Some themes include math and science, performing arts, gifted and talented and college preparatory. Magnet schools generate great enthusiasm in their cities, with governmental and business organisations often touting them as city assets much in the manner of museums, baseball parks and historical sites.

The very fact of magnet school popularity, status and educational value has also presented many school districts with a problem; that is, the vocal dissatisfaction from those who *cannot* gain access to the limited seats in the magnets. In Milwaukee, Wisconsin, where I served as superintendent of schools, parents who did not get their choices of magnet schools referred to themselves as 'lottery losers', hardly the effect support-starved public schools were looking for.

In response to this problem, some school systems that were famous for magnet schools began exploring broader systems of school choice. In its study on school choice in 1993, The Carnegie Foundation for the Advancement of Teaching's Special Report entitled *School Choice* recognized three school systems that had embraced parental choice as the mode for all schools in the district. Given that these systems were also concerned with the issue of racial desegregation, the only limits placed on parent choice were availability of seats and racial balance. The systems of Cambridge, Massachusetts, Montclair, New Jersey and District 4 of the New York City Public Schools were identified as systems that had successfully, and equitably, implemented system-wide choice programs for at least a decade or more. All three districts had established reputations as being responsive to parent demands for diverse programming *and* for promoting access to enhanced educational opportunities for poor and minority students.

Somewhat problematical, however, even the three highly-touted Systems barely demonstrated increased student performance superior to that of traditional school systems. In an article I co-authored in the Winter, 1994 edition of the *Journal of Negro Education* entitled *'Public School Choice: Implications for African-American Students'*, I reported that data was insufficient to determine the benefits derived from school choice for Black students, although initial data (what there is!) continues to make me positive for choice's potential for school reform.

If increased achievement is an elusive goal for school choice, itself a recent and ever-changing phenomenon, what accounts for the persistent demand for, and popularity of this educational innovation? I would argue that three reasons exist: educational, political and economic. With regard to education, I have spoken of the near-universal concern about the dire condition of America's urban public schools. The broader context reveals that few of America's school children perform at academically high levels. According to the National Assessment of Educational Progress, approximately 5% of the country's school children perform competitively at the highest levels with their peers from other industrialized countries in four major subject areas. We don't compare favorably with any advanced nation!

Such conditions have heightened the demand for school reform, including greater flexibility in school choice. Each year for the past 26 years, Phi Delta Kappa, a national professional fraternity in education, has commissioned the Gallup Organisation to conduct a *Poll of the Public's Attitudes Toward the Public Schools.* In the poll respondents have consistently supported greater choice in the public schools (70 out of 100 %), although the support diminishes sharply when choice is proposed for private or parochial schools (45 - 50%). The important issue here is that respondents clearly favor *more* choice in their selection of schools. Why? I would answer with alarming statistics from the PDK/Gallup poll - 51% of the respondents indicate that the nation's public schools have gotten worse while only 16% thought that they had improved! America's schools were seen as violent, lacking in discipline and fiscal resources, drug-ridden and as having questionable standards and quality of education. Couple these findings with a perception (and sometimes reality) that large public school systems have large, insensitive bureaucracies that stifle creativity and innovation and are also hostile to parents, and you have the climate for greater school choice within and without the public school system. I find the logic in this position to be compelling.

The political rationale is somewhat more complex. The local political environment has become more supportive of school choice in the public and private sectors as local communities again experience an awakening of a sense of power: some communities within our cities are largely African-American and Hispanic, groups largely outside the power elite but with children now in the majority in most large urban school systems in America: These communities are increasingly seeking greater voice in school governance at district and school levels, supporting school choice within the system and when the system is unyielding, responding to opportunities to open their own schools if other forms of public support are available, and sometimes when not.

The national political scene has sectors which support the above but may have a different agenda. While community activists and choice supporters may be liberal or conservative, Democratic, Republican or non-voting, the group that I am now discussing is overwhelmingly Republican, conservative, Christian and white. Their agenda ranges from public tax support in the form of vouchers for private and parochial school tuition to the abolition of the public system itself. While my comments about either group may sound pejorative depending on where you are on the political spectrum, I merely mean to demonstrate that for different groups and for very different reasons, school choice has many advocates and unlikely alliances that have energized more communities to action than the other reforms combined.

The best example of these forces coming together is found in the Milwaukee, Wisconsin Public Schools: The Milwaukee Public Schools has more school choice than any other school system in the United States:

- an award-winning magnet school system designed by parents and educators;
- a community process whereby citizens and groups could set the themes for new schools (the first public Waldorf, African-American, Gardner);
- an open enrolment system that allows students to enrol in any school in the district;
- an inter-district enrolment plan with twenty-three surrounding suburban school districts;
- contracts with private, community-based schools for student slots in kindergarten/day care and alternative high schools for dropouts;
- some neighborhood preference for student assignment to build local community allegiance to schools; and
- classes at local colleges for advanced placement credit.

Despite this menu of school diversity and choice, advocates from the African-American community and liberal Democratic political leaders combined with Republicans and far-right groups to support legislation that eventually passed in the state legislature for a pilot program for education vouchers in the city of Milwaukee. Up to one thousand low income students are eligible to attend private, non-sectarian schools, with tuition paid from the Milwaukee school district's state financial aid: These schools, many of which had long contractual relationships with MPS, and exist mainly on dissatisfaction with the responsiveness of the system. Long impoverished, they now have a stable revenue source and *several* new local and national constituencies. Milwaukee has the only education voucher system in the U.S.

The final reason for the attention given for the expansion of school choice in the U.S. is economic. The past five years has seen a proliferation of private companies that offer to run schools for public systems for a fee. Companies such as The Edison Project, Educational Alternatives, Inc., and Public Strategies Corporation have contracted with mostly urban school systems (performance incentives and profit margins intact) to do what the public systems themselves seem unable or unwilling to do: improve student achievement. Initially, some companies sought to be totally independent of the public sector. Faced with the need for adequate (and expensive) facilities, the necessity for exorbitant tuition, accusations of elitism and a lack of investors, most have sought to create 'private/public ventures' with school systems. In some cases, the firms have been hired to run the entire system themselves - EAI in Hartford, Connecticut and, briefly, in Duluth, Minnesota and Public Strategies in Minneapolis, Minnesota. This 'privatization' of public schools is too new to evaluate, as are most of the choice initiatives in the U.S: The interest in participation is significant as school boards and superintendents scramble to answer the criticisms levelled at their systems. Not to engage in or consider the public/private ventures is seen as being behind the curve of cutting-edge school reform.

Additionally, some of the firms that are willing to provide educational services (AEI, Public Strategies) also promise to more efficiently manage the large school budgets (which can total in the millions, even billions of dollars), clean and maintain buildings (no mean feat in a nation with $112 billion in deferred school maintenance), and introduce and manage administrative and educational technology (even Walt Disney, hopefully with better results than EuroDisney).

The public/private ventures are not just found at the local level. As more governors and state legislatures enter the choice debate, firms have been able to respond to recent charter school initiatives in states as diverse as California, Minnesota and Massachusetts. The concept of charters is deliciously simple: through a state's department for education, opportunities are posted for individuals, groups, firms or other entities to apply for a charter to run their own school(s). Applicants must generally present a philosophy, education plan, admissions procedure and evaluation design to be considered. If selected, awardees receive funds (generally district per-pupil-cost) to run the schools, freed from any local restrictions or union obligations: their sole responsibilities are to their constituents and to the state. The Edison Project has been extremely responsive to the charter opportunity; most charters, however, have gone to community groups or teachers.

Regardless of the reason, educational, political or economic, school choice has invigorated the school reform debate from the schoolhouse to the White House, from the classroom to the boardroom, and from community groups to political and business entities. Why? I think it is due to a *perceived* potential or promise that choice brings to *both* the reform debate and the community empowerment effort in the U.S., with the failure of other institutions (the possible exception being the church) to continue to serve and inspire the disenfranchised in our cities. Despite public education's current problems, the promise of universal education serving to enable social and economic mobility *does* continue to inspire my fellow citizens. You and I know that the promise has been largely unfulfilled; that it has been fulfilled at all is a minor miracle.

So we continue to see an increase in the number of children who are largely school-dependent, not just for education but for food, health services, moral and career guidance. In largely poor and increasingly abandoned inner cities, schools are also used as social service and adult education centers for students' parents and the surrounding community. When public schools are not perceived as fulfilling their educational and community functions, citizens turn to parochial or private schools or open their own struggling schools. Schools are the embodiment of educational and life enhancement opportunities for our citizens. For that reason, they *are* important. The desire to attend, support and/or create schools is essential to an understanding of the power of the school choice movement in American cities.

Let me use my home state of Massachusetts and the city of Boston as an example of the power of the new charter school movement. In 1993, the Massachusetts legislature negotiated with the Governor to pass the *second* educational reform act in the past ten years. Amid such 'reforms' as a core curriculum, the abolition of tenure for teachers and administrators, stricter certification requirements and a *small* increase in local aid, was a provision for funding charter schools. According to the legislation, charter schools are defined as:

> ...independent schools created within a community to serve as a center of innovation and educational leadership and to attract students from within the district. A charter school is established by parents, teachers or in some cases, a corporate or philanthropic/non-profit organization - not by school administrators or a school committee.. a charter school, once established, remains administratively and financially independent from any school district.. and will be open to all students regardless of their residence.

The legislation goes on to say:

The purposes for establishing charter schools are:

1. to stimulate the development of innovative programs within public education;
2. to provide opportunities for innovative learning and assessments;
3. *to provide parents and students with greater options in choosing schools within and outside their school districts* (my emphasis);
4. to provide teachers with a vehicle for establishing schools with alternative, innovative methods of educational instruction and school structure and management;
5. to encourage performance-based educational programs; and

6. to hold teachers and administrators accountable for students' 'educational outcomes'.

In the words of former US. Secretary of Education Terrel Bell who, arguably, can he considered the father of the school reform movement with his commissioning of *A Nation at Risk:*

> ...the charter school idea has emerged as possibly the most promising innovation (in school reform). The concept is simple: Create independent legal entities, charter schools, and give them the authority to operate schools as autonomous organizations with freedom to experiment and test new and creative solutions... (1995)

Hundreds of inquiries about charter school applications were received by the Massachusetts Secretary of Education; sixty-four applications were submitted: In the Spring of 1994, fourteen charters were granted with a range of themes from the Community Day Charter School, stressing a sense of 'grass roots' community and a partnership between parents, teachers and community agencies, to the Renaissance Charter School, a collaboration between The Edison Project and the Horace Mann Foundation focusing on rigorous basic skill instruction, acquisition of a second language and technological literacy. On Sunday, March 26, 1995, the headline on the front page of the Boston Globe read, 'Applicants Flood Charter School Rolls.' The article states that 'Parents across Massachusetts are so hungry for a different type of education for their children that they are swamping the state's as-yet-untested charter schools with applications.'
    The reasons cited included:

'It's almost like sending your child to a private school.'

'I like the concept (of charter schools) because the emphasis is on thinking.'

'It offers so much more than public schools can, because of the public schools' money problems and being locked into the union contracts.'

When confronted with the experimental, untested nature of charter schools, one parent quipped, 'To me, I'm experimenting when I go to the public school, too.'

This Spring, thirty-five applications were submitted and seven accepted with a similar range and diversity in thematic content. By the way, the commonwealth will fund a total of 25 charters with decisions on further expansion anticipated in 1997. I currently serve on the board of advisors of one of the new charter schools, the Benjamin Banneker Charter School, which (ironically) serves 'those minority, low-income and disadvantaged children who are under-served by the Cambridge Public schools...', the system where I was Superintendent for four years! This school also had the endorsement of the current Mayor of Cambridge who is also the president of the Cambridge school board.

The new charter schools are primarily located in the cities of eastern Massachusetts where underfunded school systems are struggling in mostly antiquated facilities to educate a more diverse population of students than elsewhere in the commonwealth. The cities also have remnants of the political machines that control both city and, to a lesser extent, school governance. Educational reform, and especially charter schools, are designed to wrest control from these very governments and their attendant bureaucracies and give it to citizens. While the bulk of reform legislation attempts to change school systems and the manner in which they conduct the business of education, charter schools deliberately bypass the bureaucracy of the systems (but not of the commonwealth), and encourage local residents to experiment with innovative school designs in the hope that the local school systems will 'learn' from successful charter models and incorporate those practices in the larger public systems. Additionally, it is hoped that citizens who have been shut out of the public process of schooling or whose children have been under-served by public schools will reinvest themselves in the educational process by starting or supporting charter schools in their communities. One impact of the charter school process can be seen in the increased willingness of some public school districts to experiment with similar models, either out of a desire to better serve their students or in enlightened self-interest. Whatever the reason, the cities of Lawrence and Lowell, Massachusetts have contracted with the Edison Project to run some of their schools.

Contracting

The Boston Public Schools, sitting under the gaze of the state legislature, has been forced to fulfil the promise of school reform issued to its citizens six years ago. In 1989, the Boston Public Schools, already providing significant choice of schools to parents and students in its controlled choice program, signed a 'reform' contract with the Boston Teachers Union which, among other innovations, promised:

> ...to establish innovative pilot schools...the purpose of which is to establish and provide models of educational excellence which will help to foster widespread educational reform throughout all Boston Public Schools. The parties hope to dramatically improve the educational learning environment and thereby improve student performance.

This 'promise' went unfulfilled during the life of that first contract and the next until initiation of the charter/commonwealth legislation, which provided for up-to-five charter schools in Boston. Boston school officials even attempted to close their only true 'innovative' school, Fenway Middle College Program, due to the antipathy of two successive superintendents. Ironically, Fenway applied for and was granted charter status and was reluctantly preparing to move outside the public system. Rightfully embarrassed, BPS signed another contract with the BTU in June, 1994, once again endorsing the creation of six pilot schools. By September, educators, cultural organizations, business leaders and community groups submitted seventeen proposals for pilot schools, with six applications accepted by last October. These schools will open in September, 1995. Joining Fenway will be the Boston Arts Academy, Downtown Evening Academy, The Health Careers Academy, Lyndon Elementary School (emphasizing thematic learning and team teaching) and the Young Achievers Science and Mathematics School. All of the schools will be exempt from district regulations and BTU contract requirements provided they meet 'sound educational practice (whatever that is) and conform to court orders and state and federal laws.'

In fact, charter schools, Boston's pilot schools and the privatization effort may signal a new *contracting* model of school choice. Contracting, as defined in the new book *Reinventing Public Education* by Hill, Pierce and Guthrie:

> builds upon the charter school movement but would extend the autonomy granted to these schools (about 140 nationwide) to all schools. Under contracting, school boards would no longer directly manage schools but would contract with independent organizations to run them.

Like charter schools,

> contracting allows schools to be operated by a variety of public and private organizations, based on school-specific contracts that would define each school's mission, guarantee public funding, ensure accountability, and maintain the credibility of public education in the United States.

I agree with Hill et al's positive assessment of charters and contracting. Moreover these approaches avoid the divisive and seemingly unsolvable issues raised by the voucher, and possibly religious (parochial) school, debate *and* permit, even encourage, the widest range of choice and public/private collaborations. Additionally, there is a public *accountability* to those served and to those who pay tax support. The contracting agents, school boards or state agencies would limit their roles to 'evaluate proposals, let and manage contracts, and ensure that contractors deliver on their promises.' As Hill indicates, that leaves contractors time to pay unrelenting attention to the quality of instruction and learning in the lowest performing schools. As I have discussed in my Massachusetts examples, just the existence of charter legislation can force school systems to be more open and responsive to constituents, providing more thematic choice for the diverse learning needs of school-dependent children. Given all of the forms taken by school choice in America, I currently believe that charter schools and contracted schools have the most value and promise.

Before I close, I would like to share some concerns about the proliferation of choice in the U.S. In my country I am seen as a choice advocate except by those who support unfettered vouchers. As superintendent of two systems with cutting-edge choice programs - controlled choice in Cambridge and vouchers in Milwaukee - I have learned some lessons which I would like to share with you. I would recommend that these lessons be studied and appropriate conditions developed in response to their impact at the local level. My comments are derived from the premise that choice advocates have no more right to needlessly or recklessly experiment with the educational lives of children than our traditional counterparts. I call these my principles of implementation and they are in a constant state of evolution. I hope that you will add to their definition and growth during our discussion today.

1. First is a Community dialogue, much like the one we are having here, commitment and political endorsement of school choice. The commitment should be built on a sense of equity for all children and a belief in the educability of all children. A community commitment should not be based simply on the desires of the middle or upper class but on the belief that all children can learn, given appropriate conditions, sufficient resources, well-trained teachers, supportive parents and community. The community should also commit that school choice will be used to bring students of different backgrounds, races and classes together rather than keep them in separate enclaves.

2. The second condition is careful strategic planning for the choice proposal using the latest research and best available practice; a well-thought-out plan should be subjected to full public debate. Advocates and detractors have the responsibility for explaining their proposals and counter-proposals and for examining the impact of their claims for those who would be clients. Full public debate would enable those clients to appraise the value of school choice and see how it relates to other goals and aspirations of the community.

3. Choice plans should be required to make full public disclosure of student outcomes. If we are to believe that choice is a vehicle for school improvement, we must accept responsibility to insure that the plans will guarantee learning outcomes for all

children. Choice schools at least must be the equivalent, if not better, than existing schools.

4. Fourth is the issue of access in establishing schools and systems of choice.

a)   Equal access to choice schools must be provided by ensuring that information on the programmatic opportunities is available to all clients. In the United States poor and minority communities (especially linguistic minority communities) do not receive the same information as majority communities, nor do they always receive information in the same manner. Such information isolation must be eliminated. In the article I authored in *Public Schools by Choice* I describe the Cambridge, Massachusetts model for reaching these parents. Cambridge created a public information center and hired parent liaisons - parents of current students - to help provide information on the systems' schools for prospective parents. In addition, parent liaisons served as advocates for parent concerns in the individual schools and contacted parents on a regular basis with information on school events and teacher concerns. Parent liaisons also helped school officials in translating official documents, report cards and other school information for linguistic minority parents. Parent liaisons, Cambridge school administrators and teachers visited laundromats, welfare offices, housing projects and other non-traditional locations to fully inform poor and minority parents of opportunities afforded them in the schools.

b)   Another access concern must be the careful establishment of anti-discrimination guidelines for schools in the public sector.

c)   There must be economic access. Students must be able to access programs without additional cost to them or their parents. This means the provision of transportation, supplies necessary for participation in thematic programs requiring special equipment, and supportive after-school programs for those students who may have been transported out of their neighborhood.

d)   We must insure an absolute integrity of assignment of youngsters to choice schools if there is an oversubscription of these schools. That means that there will be no violation of the principles of fair selection of students for schools, regardless of their parents' power or influence.

e) Additionally, at least in the United States, there must be an adherence to existing desegregation standards or consideration of the development of new standards to promote desegregation of choice schools.

5. In establishing standards and outcomes one must also consider how to publicly report those outcomes. Data should be disaggregated by race, sex, geographical area and social/economic levels so that one can determine whether on not choice is benefiting all students equally.

6. Plan for healthy collaboration between choice, public and private schools, not the free marketplace uncertainty promoted by some choice advocates. Schools should not compete for basic resources but for new opportunities and new resources. So-called 'good' schools can assist in the development of new schools as they attempt to become schools of choice. This is now being discussed for the first time in the US. between elite private schools and public schools.

7. Safety nets must exist for those who cannot get into their schools of choice. This can happen by:

a) Replication - duplication of extremely popular thematic programs;

b) Waiting lists that enable students to enrol in their original schools of choice when room is available;

c) Fair appeals for extraordinary or emergency situations;

d) Sibling preferences to keep families together;

e) Neighborhood preference if space allows.

8. The development of schools will initially demand additional resources. While schools can always use money more wisely, it takes additional money to establish new programs.

9. As much attention should be placed on teacher selection as student selection. An additional benefit of creating schools of choice, those which are largely thematic in nature, is that you have the ability to match teaching styles with thematic content and student learning styles. This enhances teacher creativity and reduces morale problems due to incompatibility of faculty members with the direction of the school's parents and students.

10. Careful attention must be paid to the coordination between school choice and the educational goals of the community. Especially important as you move toward the systems of choice is sufficient training for parents and teachers on a shared decision-making model as well as quality development programs for staff and curriculum.

Finally, we must all ask ourselves whether the benefits of school choice are potentially stronger than the current outcomes presently exhibited by public schools. I would argue that the indicators appear strong enough to recommend the adoption of school choice in our urban districts over the continuation of the failed practices of unfocused neighborhood schools, an inadequate number of innovative magnet schools and a limited number of effective public schools.

In the words of the late Ronald Edmunds, one of the founders of the school effectiveness movement in the United States:

> We can whenever and wherever we choose to successfully teach all children whose schooling is of interest to us. We already know more than we need in order to do this. Whether we do must finally depend on how we feel about the fact that we haven't so far.

Financing Free Education

Dr Rudolf Mees

The motto of my short introductory lecture today is: In practice it
will work, in theory never. This is the principle behind French
management, as I was reading yesterday.

The choice of methods of finance available to education mirrors
to some extent the views held *about* education. Is the State the
decisive authority over the system and content of education? Or is
education primarily the responsibility of parents, (students later)
teachers and the school's administration? Or can these two be
combined?

In Holland, where I was on the National Advisory Council for
Education for 15 years, State and private schools enjoy equality of
funding from public sources. This was made law in 1920, and was
the result of a lengthy fight between the religious, or Church
schools and the state's schools. During the 1960's and 1970's in
our country the State became, in addition , responsible for the
quality of education. For this reason the State influence both on
the system and the content of education became gradually ever
greater. We may be able to discuss this later, but I can assure you
that every State, every Government that presumes to be able to
assess quality cannot do otherwise than legislate on system and
content in Education.

The battle between state - and non-state schools came to an end
in 1920. Today and in future the fight will be about who carries
real responsibility, in terms of pedagogical aims, for the content of
education.

Almost all over the world we now stand at the beginning of this
battle. In Holland over 60% of schools are organised on a private
legal basis. The market share of state schools is decreasing all the
time. This is another reason why the State requires ever greater

control of educational system and content, because it is unfortunately (and cannot be otherwise) a partisan force on behalf of its own state schools. This strengthening of state control will reach a point where the execution of the curriculum (as defined by the State) will be highly decentralised. Each school will enjoy apparent autonomy. The entire day-to-day burden of running a school will be pushed under the category of this so-called school autonomy. But just *what* is to be carried out will be determined from outside the school. No other form can be taken under state control.

Parallel to these changes, the finances, hitherto dealt with in a general manner (though requiring horrendously detailed accounting, down to every last pencil) will in future be handled differently - namely with a lump sum. This means a firm contract calculated per pupil. The contract can be varied according to school type. Each school is thereby made responsible for itself, for the balancing of its books, and also for its own everyday running, governing and teaching costs. I can assure you that here is a whole new world waiting to be discovered...

Private schools can in addition ask for limited parental contributions almost always means-related, as is usual in Holland, and normally non tax-deductible. The methods of financing education mentioned have in common that they finance the supply of lessons, however directly or indirectly planned by the State. Whatever one wants to offer in addition to this (let us say 10% of the budget) can then be paid for privately. This happens in Montessori, Steiner-Waldorf, Jena Plan schools and suchlike, as also in the so-called Church schools.

Financing education by means of a voucher or coupon scheme - a theme addressed this morning - can be seen as realising the provision of free choice as far as the system and curriculum content are concerned for parents and students. 'Supply Finance' is widely available, not only in Holland. It has yet to be discovered in Britain, though the NHS is a clear case of it.

'Supply - Finance' is by definition uncontrollable. Whatever is on offer will spread, making ever greater demands on state resources.

In Holland, education funding stands at around 25 billion guilders annually, and is second only to Social Security funding. Here I would like to add that industry contributes annually around one third of the state funds (c. 7 billion guilders p.a.) required for further education training. The Banks, an area where I have been involved, pay around 6% of the total sum of salaries required to train staff. So, to recap, 'Supply Finance' can hardly be controlled.

'Demand Finance', however, is much easier to handle because responsibility for using this money no longer lies with the State (the 'Supplier') but the results of having asked for funding land as it were, directly in the demanders' treasury.

Whatever schools need in addition to what public funds can provide can then be supplemented by (albeit limited) tax deductible contributions. I will enlarge on this a little later.

A voucher system is one where each child, and later each young person, receives a right. It means, translated into financial terms, that each child enjoys the right to be educated. This right to education can be thought of in terms of an Education Bank, a bank into which the public pay their 'obligation' and hand over responsibility for the use and distribution of these funds to those people - adults, citizens - responsible in our society. In this way a healthy division between state funding and control of public resources can come about. So, although the State provides the basic taxation mechanism for channelling the funds, yet it regards this money as belonging to citizens for the education of their children and young people. In other words, it would not go into the general pot, over which ministers are so prone to haggle for control.

I once heard a lecture on historical development in England and Holland. We had Kings and Queens (and still do) who tended to be somewhat wasteful. We then invented parliaments, first in England in order to control the Monarchy. Unfortunately most countries have dispensed with kings! Now Parliament plays King. And, regrettably, no one now controls Parliament.

In Education, three levels or phases can be recognised. The first, where education is both a right and a duty for parents. This covers the ages 4-16. The second is a phase where education becomes a right and a responsibility for the young people or students participating (let's say between ages 16-25). A third phase applies to higher or further education, where education becomes an opportunity.

The first phase can be financed with vouchers or coupons and, where necessary, supplemented with inversely taxable, limited parental contributions. I say inversely, which may sound slightly odd, but the way it works in today's income tax system is for less well-off people to be offered less financially rewarding tax concessions than their wealthier counterparts. For this reason it is a reversed or inverted figure for education contribution purposes.

The second phase can be financed in the form of, for example, 50% vouchers and 50% tax-deductible contributions. This is merely by way of example.

In the third phase, finance could take the form of, say, 20% vouchers, 80% tax deductible contribution (inverted, as mentioned earlier).

If, for example, a student or child were to miss a year, for whatever reason, the right to study could in a sense be banked, as in the case of a savings account, with the 'Education Bank'. It could then be redeemed at a later date. This would allow one to remain independent of a budget that might, by then, have over-extended itself. Within this framework, the role of the state is limited to the formulation of rights, duties and obligations and the organisation of funding, (insofar as this is necessary; for where this takes place through an Education bank, such burdens are the task of responsible, qualified citizens).

The system and content of education has in this way become the responsibility of parents, teachers and, later, of students themselves - and, of course, also of schools' management. Teachers are, after all, mature people. Students are certainly grown up, school management likewise. We assume all parties to maintain integrity throughout, so what, one may ask, can the state system add to this? Integrity, maturity, expert knowledge in given fields? To my mind all it would contribute are the negative effects of bureaucracy.

The funding of education by vouchers would be raised on a *request* basis and visibly carried by mature and qualified people willingly holding such responsibility. However, a mighty revolution is implied in all this for lessons themselves, for the Curriculum. Because today in the main - and many excellent teachers are excluded from what I am about to say - teachers have unfortunately become civil servants, bound to carry out

Government instructions. I discovered in Holland that the greatest resistance to a real and fundamental change from Supply to Demand Funding comes not so much from the State but rather from within the ranks of teachers themselves. For it is here that the reason for what I might call the unconscious routine of lessons is hauled into the light of scrutiny. Teachers will be required to learn how to become pedagogical entrepreneurs. I can assure you that high quality lessons without pedagogically entrepreneurial input will never, never be achieved. Secondly, the world of the classroom is the only one in which I have ever encountered people who maintain that they themselves (on behalf of the State) are capable of defining what quality is! Anywhere else in the world it is accepted that quality is defined by the consumer, not the supplier.

Only an education capable of constantly renewing itself, and orientated towards the future renewal of society can make reality out of responsibility. On the one hand education will be able to accompany the changes and upheavals in the world. On the other hand - and more importantly - it will be an education which can equip our children not only with what they are required to know, but also with the means of nurturing their own inherent *development potential* and thus leading society forwards.

The tragedy of state control- and we must be extremely sober here- is that what lies behind state control is, for the greatest part, the economy. The economy, (stated) quite objectively, has no other primary aim than to condition young people in accordance with the needs of the economy - as perceived in today's terms. The fact that the economy, on closer inspection, is also finding out that today's requirements alone are woefully short-sighted is quite a recent development.

The struggle I portrayed for freedom of curriculum rages between two extremes. On the one side we have the tendency to state control which must inevitably lead to all freedom, mobility and development potential within education ceasing to exist. The other side, in the form of the economy's tendency to focus exclusively on its own short-term needs and gains, and this in turn exerts pressure on the curriculum to produce co-workers for industry equipped with qualities defined by today's requirements.

The task of education is none other than a *cultural* task. And culture, as I am sure all here will understand, can never, by very definition, become a function of the state, or the economy. Culture must be able to function independently as a source of fertilisation, as inspiration for both state and economy.

I have tried to indicate how finance can be a means of opening chinks of opportunity, a means called upon by mature people who want to carry responsibility for the future.

I also mentioned that, to some extent, methods of finance reflect what people demand, rightly or wrongly, of a cultural activity.

At the level of discussion it is important to bear in mind that a change in funding cannot of itself bring about a resolution of the battles I outlined to you. They must be fought on a different level. Financial solutions will then materialise. However, a fight for freedom can never take as its starting point the premise: 'I will fight when I have the money.' If that were to be the case, that battle is lost before it is begun.

In conclusion I would like to say that I have been glad to develop, differently, on an angle I spoke of two years ago in Bern. Differently in that, on English soil, in Britain, I believe there to be a unique opportunity available. Due to ancient traditions that have held sway longer here than elsewhere in Europe (on the Continent, as you like to call it here) Britain may be able to avoid some of the terrible mistakes we have unfortunately experienced in Europe. In other words, even if these mistakes were to be made (and it could happen), one could at least remind oneself that they are only a step on a path that *could* lead towards completely new and different solutions.

Translated by Christiana Bryan and Martyn Rawson

Educational Freedom across Europe

Fiona Carnie,
Human Scale Education

Children are entitled to education and to freedom in education. These are fundamental human rights which between 1948 and 1990 were expressed in no less than fourteen international declarations and conventions.[1] The Universal Declaration of Human Rights (1948) states that 'parents have a prior right to choose the kind of education that shall be given to their children'. More recently the European Parliament Declaration of Fundamental Rights and Freedoms (1989) states that 'there shall be freedom in education. Parents shall have the prior right to make provision for such education in accordance with their religious and philosophical convictions'

Freedom in education has two main aspects [2] and the situation concerning each varies greatly across Europe:

the right to the free development of the individual which entails the need for a diversity of educational provision;

the right of those involved in schools (parents, teachers, students) to participate in decision making about the school.

The European Survey Map produced annually by the European Forum for Freedom in Education[3] reports on the situation concerning freedom in education in twenty six European countries. The purpose of this article is to draw on these reports in order to identify trends in the current state of educational freedom across Europe.

The right to free development of the individual

For parents to be able to choose the kind of education which is best suited to their child, there needs to be a variety of schools to choose from. As Michael Young has said 'it is because children are not alike, their parents are not alike, their interests are unlike and their needs are unlike that they need different kinds of schools' [4]. The free development of the individual which entails the development of his or her own abilities and personality can best happen when a child attends a school which is suited to his or her own needs.

The concept of free development of the individual is an unusual one for people in the UK. It is acknowledged by the independent sector where schools like Summerhill can flourish, but not in the state system where uniformity of provision prevails.

Education systems which concentrate on uniformity of provision generally do so on the grounds of equality of opportunity. Such systems (for example in the UK) have to be centrally controlled to facilitate this uniformity. Central control militates against flexibility however and this makes it much more difficult for schools to respond to the differing needs of individuals.

The commitment to a system which provides different kinds of schools varies from country to country. Two of the most libertarian education systems in Europe - those in Denmark and Holland - allow groups of parents and /or teachers to establish independent schools, and provide funding for them. Both countries have a wide range of schools, such as Christian, Jewish, Muslim, Montessori, Steiner and small parent-run schools alongside the state-run (maintained) schools. These schools have the right to exist and are given state funding because of a commitment by successive governments in those countries to real choice for parents about the kind of education they want for their children. The governments recognise that a diversity of educational provision is required to achieve this. Making funding available allows a variety of schools to be set up. Such schools (which are called private schools because of their independence of the state) receive 85% of running costs from the government in Denmark and 100% in Holland.

State support for independent schools (see footnote) is becoming increasingly widespread and in recent years legislation has been passed in Sweden, Finland, Norway, Germany and parts of Switzerland allocating government funds to such schools. In Sweden for example, the number of independent schools has quadrupled in the last three years from 60 to 250 (and a further 300 applications for funding are awaiting approval). These schools receive 75% of their costs from government funds. They are not allowed to charge fees although voluntary contributions are permitted. In Finland and Norway, non-state schools have received similar financial support from the government since 1991. In Germany state support for independent schools is well established and schools which meet the criteria laid down by the government are entitled to around 80% of their costs.

The situation in the UK is markedly different. It has more in common with the systems of France, Italy and Spain. These all operate on a more centralised basis and none of them provide state funding for non-state schools. The current Conservative administration in the UK professes to support choice and diversity in education. Yet with a prescriptive national curriculum taught in all maintained schools and a complete absence of funding for new and innovative independent schools, the reality is the opposite. Independent fee-paying schools have the right to exist in the UK but the level of fees means that they offer a choice only to the minority of parents who can afford them.

In this respect the UK lags behind not only the liberal Western European countries already mentioned but also many in Eastern Europe. Prior to the opening up of Eastern Europe which came with 'glasnost' schools other than those funded and run by the State were illegal. However, many of these countries are now seeing a growing private sector of schools which are independently run but in receipt of some state funding. In the Czech Republic and in Poland for example, the state provides a significant proportion of running costs for independent schools - 65% in the Czech Republic and 50% in Poland. In both of these countries around 3% of schools are now self-governing. In other countries such as Slovenia and Croatia, new legislation which will give private state-supported schools the right to exist, is being prepared.

Genuine choice within a diverse system can only be made available if new schools are openly encouraged and publicly funded. Such a policy also fosters the innovation and experimentation which is needed in education in order to identify ways forward for learning. New approaches are needed because technological advance, environmental pressures and economic constraints mean that society is in a continual process of change. Education needs to keep pace with these developments in order to equip young people to live in our rapidly-evolving world.

If the right for these schools to exist and be publicly funded is accepted the question of the level of state funding needs to be addressed. Holland is the only European country that funds its private schools on the same basis as the state run schools. In all of the other countries mentioned the schools themselves have to raise a proportion of their funds, ranging from 15% in Denmark to 50% in Poland. The majority of these schools raise the extra money through parental contributions (voluntary or otherwise) and/or donations from charitable foundations. This raises questions about the elitism of these schools. If parents who cannot afford to contribute financially to their childrens' education are left without any choice, then educational freedom is compromised.

There are different ways of funding diversity (examples of which are discussed in the articles by Mees and Peterkin) and it is incumbent on governments to find an equitable way to do so. This duty is recognised in the European Parliament Resolution on Freedom in Education in the European Community (1984) which states that "In accordance with the right to freedom of education Member States shall be required to provide the financial means whereby this right can be exercised in practice, and to make the necessary public grants to enable schools to carry out their tasks and fulfil their duties under the same conditions as in corresponding State establishments..."

The right to participate in decision making

Equally important as the right to establish schools which meet the differing needs of children is the right of parents, teachers and children to participate in decisions about how their school is run. For schools to be able to develop and to have the capacity to respond to the needs of the children in their care they need freedom of organisation and freedom over their curriculum. This requires the involvement of teachers, parents and children to produce an appropriate curriculum. By including children in this process they learn what is meant by democracy through active participation in decision making. Children can only develop responsibility if they are given responsibility and so this involvement is an important part of their education.

Most parents and schools would want the state to have an advisory and inspection role to ensure that basic standards are met and the rights of children are protected. The challenge for governments is to exercise these functions without interfering in detailed decisions that should be made by those directly involved with the school.

There is a move towards greater freedom in this field in a number of European countries. The majority of governments in Eastern Europe are moving away from a tightly controlled and rigid curriculum to a situation which gives much more freedom to teachers. They are hampered in this, however, by the fact that, on the whole, the teachers who are teaching now are the same as those who taught under the more repressive regimes prior to 'glasnost'; they cannot change their authoritarian methods overnight. A more libertarian approach requires different methods which have to be learned. Exchanges have been set up between teachers in Western and Eastern Europe to assist with this development. It is clear however that it will be a long, slow process.

Romania provides a good example of positive educational change in this area. Recent legislation makes it possible for groups, classes or whole schools to be based on alternative educational ideas. If the majority of parents and teachers involved in an institution or part of an institution vote in favour of an alternative methodology, the school is allowed to alter its approach accordingly. In this way, both direct involvement in decision-making and a consequent variety of educational methodologies are being introduced into the state system. Furthermore, in 1994 the Ministry of Education set up a Commission of Alternative Education to monitor developments.

Other Eastern European countries however, (Estonia, for example) link the question of curricular freedom with funding and demand that, as in the UK, any school which receives state funding teaches the national curriculum.

Finland is an example of a country which recognises the unique position of teachers and parents to develop an appropriate curriculum. Recent reforms have attempted to strengthen the decision-making powers of local councils and schools and, since

Autumn 1994, the state has handed over to individual schools the right to design their own curriculum. Even before 1994 Montessori and Freinet methods were openly adopted within some state schools. In Austria, too, Montessori methods can be found in a number of state schools. Each region in Germany passes its own education laws and as a result there is great variation across the country. Some regions have given schools greater flexibility and autonomy to set priorities while others, notably Bavaria, maintain tight centralised control. The question of school autonomy is particularly alive in Germany at the moment where in most cases the government of each region allocates teachers to schools, rather than allowing schools to select their own. Increasing numbers of schools want this system changed.

Autonomy of schools is a key factor in educational freedom and this is recognised in a number of the international declarations (for example, the UNESCO Recommendation Concerning the Status of Teachers, 1966) which refer to freedom of teaching and the role of teachers to select the methods and material most suitable for their pupils.

Conclusion

The European Survey Map [3] has been produced annually for the past four years. With the benefit of four years' hindsight, it is possible to detect a move towards increased freedom and diversity in education in Europe, particularly in Eastern European countries. In some countries this trend has been hampered by shifts towards nationalism, changes of government or economic difficulties. It is clear, for example, that the expansion of educational freedom is threatened in many European countries by the dwindling resources allocated to education. Even in Finland the adverse financial situation accompanied by concomitant cuts in school budgets is undermining the otherwise favourable trend in educational developments. In the UK, the regressive effects of recent reforms to the education system are exacerbated by the rise in class sizes which have resulted from financial cutbacks.

There are still some European countries such as Italy, Spain, France and Greece which have little or no representation in the European Forum for Freedom in Education, and in which the situation concerning freedom of education is far from favourable.

It should be stated, however, that despite the monitoring work carried out by the Forum it is not easy to make reliable generalisations about the state of freedom in education across Europe because of the different strands involved. Perhaps the UK is the most marked example of this. Whilst it has regressed on many fronts in terms of freedom and diversity since the advent of the National Curriculum and compulsory testing, it does at least permit dissatisfied families to opt out of the system completely and educate at home - a freedom which is denied in many countries. And, for some Europeans, the right of private fee-paying schools to exist is an important one, when they live in countries which allow nothing but attendance at state run and maintained public schools.

The situation in each country is unique - culturally, historically and politically - and therefore the drive towards greater freedom will be different in each. What is clear, however, is that the UK is lagging behind many as a result of its reluctance to fund independent, innovative schools and its insistence on a prescriptive National Curriculum. Many people overseas would imagine that the advantage of a long, democratic history should place Britain well ahead in the field of freedom in education. Unfortunately the converse is true. It is way behind in terms of developing a flexible and democratic education system suitable for a rapidly changing society moving into the next millennium.

Footnote: The term private or independent school in the context of this chapter is used in the non-British sense to refer to schools which are not state controlled although they receive state funding.

Notes

1. See appendix for list of International Declarations and Conventions.
2. Siegfried Jenkner, *International Declarations and Conventions on the Right to Education and the Freedom of Education*, Info 3 Verlag, Stuttgart 1992
3. *European Survey Map 1994-5*, European Forum for Freedom in Education. 1995
4. Michael Young, *Choice in Education, Resurgence Magazine*, Hartland, Devon, September 1988.

PART II

HOW TO BUILD MORE DIVERSITY AND REAL CHOICE IN EDUCATION

Third Sector Alliance: Schools that want to join the state system

Colin Hodgetts

When so much is wrong with state schools it may seem strange that many of those that are not part of the system want to join it. They include Muslim, Seventh Day Adventist, New Christian, Steiner, and small schools belonging to the Human Scale Education movement. This is an odd collection of bedfellows, brought together to form the Third Sector Alliance in order to put pressure on the government to fund them. There is another common factor: the parents who founded these schools want to see spiritual values enshrined in them, not the materialist values that now prevail in our society. Many materialists do not understand this because they themselves attach little importance to, or even deny, the spiritual.

The parents who send children to these schools usually cannot afford to pay economic fees. The Oak Hill Trust says that the 90 or so new Christian schools do not generally select parents on the grounds of their ability to pay for private education, and public funding has become a significant issue for those in the 'reluctant private sector'. These parents do not understand why Church of England, Roman Catholic and a few Jewish schools should receive state funding and not them, a view shared by the Muslim schools and the Seventh Day Adventists. For them, and us, this is a matter of justice. And if the government is sincere in its commitment to diversity and choice, then surely it should support such schools?

Individual schools from among these groups have been applying for voluntary aided and grant maintained status with little sign of success. One huge hurdle for GM status is the detailed paperwork, including hard evidence of sustained future demand, that the Funding Agency requires. The Alliance is recommending a government-funded three-year trial period as a more appropriate way of assessing a school's viability. We also seek to challenge two criteria to which the government attaches great importance, spare places and size. The government wants to encourage new schools where there is a shortage of places, not where there is excess capacity. But if they are serious about offering parents choice then there are bound to be spare places. The school system also has to respond to an elastic birth rate.

As schools are funded on a per capita basis, this does not have to be an issue for central government. Spare capacity is surely a school's problem. In New York, where numbers are rising, there is now a shortage of places, in part because some schools took advantage of a previous drop in numbers to spread themselves. A comprehensive here might let out some of its spare square metres to a new school. Why not?

The issue of size is more complex. The received wisdom is that you need specialists to cover all the subject areas, especially at secondary level. Between 500 and 600 pupils is considered an effective minimum size to ensure specialist coverage of all subjects. Schools of 300 and fewer are definitely believed to be in trouble, and if they try and organise in the way that bigger schools do, then perhaps they are. But a school of 36, such as the Small School, Hartland, is quite a different kind of institution and you cannot predict its problems by extrapolating down. Its problems will not be ten times worse than those of a school of 360! Nor should the commitment to specialists pass unchallenged. It can be much more rewarding for a teacher to cover a handful of subject areas than to teach the same one all day. It ought not to be a problem for a reasonably educated teacher to take these to GCSE level. 'A' levels could present more difficulties, though the consensus amongst educationists, if not parents and politicians, is that there needs to be a broadening at this level.

There is yet another good reason for supporting new schools. At present there is no provision within the state sector for controlled experiment. We have in the past committed ourselves to comprehensive schools, for instance, without carrying out proper trials. Most of the government's initiatives of the past few years have been ideologically driven and have not been properly researched and tested before being implemented. New schools offer the possibility of introducing innovation in a sound and unthreatening way. They can be our test beds for good new practice.

Flaws in the system

We are going to need new models and approaches because our state system is a time bomb waiting to explode. Since Gillian Shephard became Secretary of State for Education she has sought to soothe frayed nerves and tempers by promising that there would be no more change to the school system. She hopes teachers will now settle down with the new ways and demands. Some hope! Already the parents of Oxfordshire are promising a revolt over class sizes to match the massive campaign to abolish the poll tax. That will be just the beginning. For one thing, the system is seriously underfunded, which is why class sizes are growing. We spend half, per capita of population, what the French and the Germans spend on education. Funding is a problem, as Mrs. Shephard privately admits, though she continues to mouth, with a brazen disregard for common sense, John Major's claim that class size is irrelevant. They believe that if they repeat it often enough the public will accept it as true. They are not quite lying. What their small print says is that a small increment in numbers makes no significant difference, that is, 28 instead of 26 pupils, which is probably correct. Five or ten extra pupils do, however, make a difference, as the Tennessee STAR research project has shown, and that is the sort of increase that teachers and parents are complaining about.

There are also flaws built into the system. A National Curriculum may succeed in raising standards at the bottom by forcing schools to improve provision for the slow and the bored, but it is equally likely to hold back the progress of the brightest and best. That is flaw one. Flaw two is that a state curriculum becomes rooted and therefore reluctant to move with the times. I suffered Latin long after there was any need for it because of sluggishness at university/exam board level, and that was Latin without government prescription. What sort of effort are teachers going to have to make to ensure that the National Curriculum moves with the times? Barbara Imrie draws attention to a third flaw, that loss of teacher autonomy corrupts and impoverishes the relationship between teacher and pupils, which is what pupils' learning is rooted in. The teacher loses the possibility of responding flexibly to the needs of her particular class, in a particular local context. Most of the schools that comprise the Third Sector Alliance wish to negotiate their own curricula with the DfE, and the legislation does allow for this possibility.

There are flaws in the buildings, too. Flat-roofed, glass-fronted, purpose-built comprehensives, if they were constructed more than twenty-five years ago, are entering a critical phase for the simple reason that most of the materials that went into their making have a guaranteed life of twenty years. This does not mean that they will not last much longer, but do not count on it.

The buildings are under stress and so are the teachers. It is not only the paperwork associated with the national curriculum, and having to teach larger classes, but also the strain of appraisal. On top of this, teachers feel undervalued: they no longer have any professional autonomy. Their situation is one that can easily lead to nervous breakdowns, and some, including head teachers, are experiencing this. As employers have a legal duty 'to take reasonable care to ensure that health is not placed at risk through excessive and sustained levels of stress arising from the way work is organised', heads and governors need to be careful or they could end up in court.

The system cannot survive in its present form. This is not to deny that possibly the majority of schools and the majority of teachers seem to be coping at present. This is a brave face they are exhibiting. Talk to teachers individually and you see the signs of stress. Talk to teachers who have left the profession and you will find that for them it was leave or crack up. The dis-ease is by no means an inner city problem. According to a confidential OFSTED report obtained by *The Observer*, when GCSE performance is weighted for social factors, the highest proportion of under-achieving schools, 13.5%, is in the London suburbs. They claim that 9.9% of shire schools and 9.5% of big city schools have poor results, and that schools with a significant number of Asian students do very well. So do single-sex comprehensives. (*The Observer*, 19 November, 1995)[1]

I do not want to go on rehearsing the shortcomings of our school system. Just enough to show that Mrs. Shephard's quiet life is a pipe dream. We are in for a lot more turbulence. If they do not watch out, teachers will again be blamed for system failure. What worries me most is the cavalier and arrogant way in which our political masters and mistresses impose wholesale change without adequate research, consultation or resources. When the next crisis arises they are likely to be just as insensitive in their response unless a new element can be introduced into the system.

The downside of a statistical approach and the curse of low expectations

Having seen the unfortunate consequences of changes introduced from the top by Secretaries of State from Kenneth Baker onwards, it will come as no surprise that some of us believe that top-down change is always likely to be ham-fisted. This is not true of politicians. One of the Opposition education team made it clear to me recently that new schools could not expect much of their time or attention, and neither can party backbench backwoodsmen who want the abolition of public schools and grammar schools, because the education team is preoccupied with the problems of the 25,000 schools in the state sector. They do not want to know about the trees in the wood. Such top-downers have a statistical approach to life. They are happy if 90% of schools deliver the goods, if 90% of teachers are competent and if 90% of lessons are well-taught. The individual pupil who is either very slow or very quick, and does not get what he or she needs, is merely unfortunate. This sort of approach, which works in the interests of the majority, does not work in the interest of everyone.

Actually, 90% do not get a good deal. Whereas in Germany 62% of 16-year-olds are of GCSE A-C standard in maths, science and mother tongue, and in France, 66%, in England and Wales it is only 27%. Our underachievement is, I believe, the result of low expectation. A study of the educational experiences of Japanese children at school in the UK claims that, 'in our current system, where relatively few children can achieve the highest levels of academic success, parents are conditioned to accept a higher "failure" rate.' 'British teachers accept, for the most part unquestioningly, the notion that pupils will display a wide range of abilities and aptitudes, and this expectation can become 'self-fulfilling'. They report the case of one pupil, described as 'intelligent and hard-working' who had been allocated to the lowest ability language group. 'The teacher saw no contradiction in

this because the pupil was "good for a second language learner".'
However, the expectation of most Japanese students was high and
consequently so was achievement, at least in part. This is unusual
for minority groups. Researchers 'are accustomed to finding a
vicious circle, where notions of social and educational
disadvantage lead to low expectations, in turn leading to low
achievement, thus reinforcing perceptions of disadvantage'.[2]

When I ran *Save the Children's* Vietnamese resettlement
programme we discovered that youngsters who had shown
promise in their English language lessons in reception centres were
being placed in remedial groups in the schools to which they were
sent on settlement. Their teachers reported that they were doing
well. I knew that studies of West Indian underachievement blamed
low teacher expectation and, fearing a similar failure among the
Vietnamese, set up a residential school in Bingley to get 50
youngsters through '0' levels in two years. The teachers reported
that they had never taught so fast. A crucial factor in the success
of the programme, which focused largely on the sciences, was to
teach key concepts in both English and mother tongue. I also
believe that our confidence that all these youngsters could get to
university was a significant factor in helping them to succeed.

If a system is going to meet everyone's needs then it has to start
with the individual. It has to be designed from the bottom up. It
has to allow the teacher the flexibility and the authority to respond
to the individual in the most appropriate way. This was Tolstoy's
approach. His teacher was not merely a conveyer of society's values
or a filter for culture but 'a remarkably independent and creative
artist who.. stimulates the pupil to understand those aspects of
culture that he as a teacher deems valuable' [3]. This freedom is
defined and restricted by the claims of the world around and the
pupil's need to live in it successfully post school.

Responsible teachers

Alongside the freedom goes responsibility, the responsibility to see
that the pupils in a teacher's care realise their potential. It is here
that I believe small schools can lead the way. In the first place, they
are able to get to know individual pupils well. They are then able
to tailor their teaching to meet individual need. In a large school it
is almost impossible to pin responsibility for poor pupil

performance on any individual teacher. Failure is blamed on the previous school or previous teacher or the ineptness of colleagues. Chris Woodhead, who is in charge of school inspection, believes that 15,000 teachers are not up to scratch. I am surprised that he sets such a low figure, but I suppose it depends where you take 'scratch' to be. He also says that, except in the early years, size of class is not relevant. Perhaps it is not if you have well-motivated youngsters, but if the teacher has to get them motivated then individual attention is required.

In the Hartland Small School we knew that we were responsible and could be held to that responsibility by parents and pupils. For this reason some teachers might not fancy exposing themselves by taking up a small school post. Knowing the pupil also means knowing the pupil's background. The study of Japanese children in our schools, to which I have already referred, found that teachers were not well-informed about the circumstances that had brought these youngsters to the UK nor were they aware of their daily life in the UK. Some made comparisons between Japanese and Pakistani pupils, others between Japanese and Vietnamese, both irrelevant parallels, on the basis of which they made inappropriate recommendations to parents. At Hartland Small School teachers report annually to parents in the home, thus ensuring some knowledge of it.

In all schools supporting the Alliance teachers know they are responsible and take that responsibility seriously. That is why they are teaching in such schools. They also tend to have an optimistic view of human nature which allows them to be more positive about the capabilities of their pupils. I would venture to guess that they have higher expectations than the average teacher in a state school. Government may not attach much importance to this. I heard Gillian Shephard tell Sue Lawley, on *Desert Island Discs,* of the high expectations her teachers had of her and her fellows in a school of 300. In the face of close questioning she stolidly maintained that larger schools are better because they can offer more subjects, such as two modern and two classical languages. She seemed to discount the contribution that relatively small size, which encourages close teacher contact and interest, might have had on the school's and her own success, and the possibility that in a large school pupils would not get similar individual attention.

Bringing about change

Two American professors who looked at the English school system called for greater autonomy for both teachers and schools and identified substantial autonomy as the most important condition for a successful school. Another was having a teaching head. John Chubb and Terry Moe hoped that enough schools would opt out to bring the top-down system to its knees 'and create a hybrid with lots of choice, competition and autonomy'. If the top stopped dictating, which is extremely unlikely - even David Blunkett feels it incumbent on him to pontificate on the number of hours of homework a child should do - then school quality would be in the hands of the teachers. 'The schools must be free to chart their own course, and it is parents and students - not the state - who have the primary role in holding the schools accountable.' [4] This is not achieved by putting parents on governing bodies. Such parents think and act like governors, not parents.

The massive opt out has not materialised. Change will not come by that route. Nor can we expect Ministers to refrain from interfering. Perhaps teachers could take a lead? Any teacher, or group of teachers, who wants to change a school from within faces an uphill struggle. Even with the Head on the side of change it is difficult to carry the whole staff. In the States, the Coalition of Essential Schools, founded in 1984, has supported schools that wanted to change themselves from within. A researcher told me that it is extremely difficult to achieve, in large part because of a rump of resistance amongst the staff. It would seem that the more problems a school has the more difficult it is to initiate change.

Not enough attention has been paid in the UK to the need to achieve a unity of purpose amongst staff. David Hargreaves may be right in saying that this is because schools are not open about what they are trying to do, which means teachers cannot know where they want to be. Schools do have their own agenda - there is no uniformity - and they should be bold enough to publish that which is hidden. Heads need the power to dispense with the services of those who do not share a school's vision or who do not realise it effectively. Schools are run for pupils, not for teachers, and teachers should not expect to have security of tenure. At present, the easiest way to turn a failing school around is to close and reopen it, which is, in effect, to sack the staff.

Extensive change will come only when the system starts to break down. It will be then that the importance of having alternative models both inside and outside the system will become apparent Let me tell you about the Julia Richman school in New York. It was one of a number of large, failing high schools which the Board of Education were at a loss to know how to turn around. The shooting of two pupils in a high school created a crisis that energised politicians to take radical action.

There are about twenty failing comprehensives in New York city with approximately 65,000 students on roll. These schools are 'the overwrought, overcrowded school system's safety nets for those students who have been rejected by all the schools to which they applied. Notorious for their high rates of failure and low rates of graduation - 20-40% - as well as for their squadrons of security guards manning scanners and metal detectors at the thresholds to learning, these safety net schools often entrap the most vulnerable students in a pernicious web of failure.' [5]

The Board has a scheme to replace two large New York City high schools with 12 new small schools. The small schools are being housed in the old schools' buildings. This project, called the Coalition Campus Schools Project, is part of the Board of Education's 3-year city plan to create 50 new-model high schools. 'The CCS Project hopes to transform large, troubled, comprehensive high schools into small, successful autonomous educational communities that can deliver excellent, highly-personalised education to the most vulnerable students in the school system.' [6]

The Board has been phasing out Julia Richman, a Manhattan comprehensive high school, since 1993. There is one year of students left. The Julia Richman campus plan includes four high schools, an elementary school, an infant-toddler day-care and nursery + Teen Parenting Resource Center, and a professional development institute. Each of these is autonomous. The mix will ensure that the campus is not overrun by adolescents.

The Urban Academy

I visited the Urban Academy, one of the four high schools. The Urban Academy's Co-Director and co-founder, Ann Cook, told me that it had been established for ten years but had only this year taken its place within the Julia Richman building. For seven years it had felt itself to be a Cinderella of the system. 'Historically, the Board of Education, like other large urban school systems, has responded to the need for innovation with *policy by exception* which relegates innovative schools to the periphery of the system.' [6] At least there was a place for innovative schools within the system. We do not enjoy that luxury, the wisdom of which became apparent when the Board wanted small schools for the Julia Richman campus. The Urban Academy became a model for other new schools. (The background to the introduction of innovative schools into the public sector is given by Professor Peterkin in his paper in Part I)

We sat around Ann Cook's desk in a large converted classroom that now houses the office in which each teacher has his or her desk. To get to their own common room students have to pass through the office. Some stop off at a teacher's desk for information or a chat. The staff purposely have no bolt hole. They want to be accessible and visible. They want students to see them working.

I have the impression that teachers here are both extremely dedicated and very hard-working. Avram Barlowe's timetable begins at 8 am and finishes at 6 pm. The teaching day ends just before 3 pm and the rest is devoted to meetings. Teachers take very seriously their own professional development and a commitment to collaborate, in fact, the core members of the teaching team were recruited from an in-service training programme. They also take on a parenting role and may even become a surrogate family because 'students' survival needs must be met before they can be responsive to the school's educational agenda'.

'Sharon's story illustrates how the role of staff-as-family is enacted at UA. "Urban took over where my parents left off when they died," Sharon explains. "They gave me an education every day. They made sure I got my Social Security check and [that] I knew my tenant rights. They even found me a job." UA was Sharon's fourth and last high school.' [6]

I also visited the Alternative Community School in Ithaca, best known for being the home of Cornell University. It is a middle and high school that opened in 1974. It has 260 students and a long waiting list. Enrolment is open. ACS is a 'Partnership School', one of the first ten in the state to be officially so designated in a collaborative effort with the State Education Department to bring about major reforms in secondary education throughout the state.

Here was a school, ACS, that encouraged persistent questioners, that allowed its students to make important curriculum choices, that promoted extended projects, encouraged independent and community studies and even encouraged students to use other educational facilities such as the college and the university.

No grading of students here but 'narrative evaluations', which includes an element of self-evaluation. Each student belongs to a family group which meets twice a week to work on school and personal issues. There are committees, of decision-making groups and action-oriented groups, each meeting twice weekly. Once a week there is an all-school meeting in which decision-making is vested. 'Students learn self-discipline and self-motivation through participation in self and school governance: students help design the school curriculum, design their own schedules each cycle, and through student/staff committees, help to run the school.' [8]

The principles of both these schools are those of the Coalition of Essential Schools. Behind the Coalition is Theodore R. Sizer, Professor of Education at Brown University, and before that, dean and professor at the Harvard Graduate School of Education. He says that the nine principles that have been adopted act in combination. You cannot pick-and-mix. Nor can change be brought about without a retraining of teachers, which involves more that a handful of Baker days a year. The movement is primarily a movement in pedagogy, 'in the relationship between teacher, student and the subjects of study that bring them together For example, the aphorism student-as-worker/teacher-as-coach affects everything, from the way the school adheres to the expectations of both teachers and pupils to the nature and seriousness of staff development.' [9]

Let me give you the nine principles, which should show that the thinking behind many Alliance schools, which is remarkably similar, is not some English aberration.

1. The school should focus on helping adolescents **learn to use their minds well.** Schools should not attempt to be 'comprehensive' if such a claim is made at the expense of the school's central intellectual purpose.

2. The school's goals should be simple; that each student **master a limited number of essential skills and areas of knowledge.** While these skills and areas will, to varying degrees, reflect the traditional academic disciplines, the programme's design should be shaped by the intellectual and imaginative powers and competencies that students need, rather than necessarily by 'subjects' as conventionally defined. The aphorism 'less is more' should dominate: curricular decisions should be guided by the aim of thorough student mastery and achievement rather than by an effort merely to cover content.

3. The school's **goals should apply to all students,** while the means to these goals will vary as those students themselves vary. School practice should be tailor-made to meet the needs of every group or class of adolescents.

4. **Teaching and learning should be personalised** to the maximum feasible extent. Efforts should be directed towards a goal that no teacher have direct responsibility for more than 80 students. To capitalise on this personalisation, decisions about details of the course of study, the use of students' and teachers' time and the choice of teaching materials and specific pedagogies must be unreservedly placed in the hands of the principal and staff.

5. **The governing practical metaphor of the school should be student-as-worker,** rather than the more familiar metaphor of teacher-as-deliverer-of-instructional-services. Accordingly, a prominent pedagogy will be coaching, to provoke students to learn how to learn and thus to teach themselves.

6. Students entering secondary school studies are those who can show competence in language and elementary mathematics. Students of traditional high school age but not yet at appropriate levels of competence to enter secondary school studies will be provided intensive remedial work to assist them quickly to meet these standards. **The diploma should be awarded upon a successful final demonstration of**

mastery for graduation - an 'Exhibition'. This Exhibition by the student of his or her grasp of the central skills and knowledge of the school's programme may be jointly administered by the faculty and by higher authorities. As the diploma is awarded when earned, the school's programme proceeds with no strict age grading and with no system of credits collected by time spent in class. The emphasis is on the students' demonstration that they can do important things.

7. **The tone of the school should** explicitly and self-consciously stress values of unanxious expectation ('I won't threaten you but I expect much of you') of trust (until abused) and of **decency** (the values of fairness, generosity and tolerance). Incentives appropriate to the school's particular students and teachers should be emphasised, and parents should be treated as essential collaborators.

8. **The principal and teachers should perceive themselves as generalists first** (teachers and scholars in general education) and specialists second (experts in but one particular discipline). Staff should expect multiple obligations (teacher-counsellor-manager) and a sense of commitment to the entire school.

9. Ultimate administrative and budget targets should include, in addition to **total student loads per teacher of 80 or fewer pupils, substantial time for collective planning by teachers, competitive salaries for staff and an ultimate per pupil cost not to exceed that at traditional schools by more than 10%.** To accomplish this, administrative plans may have to show the phased reduction or elimination of some services now provided students in many traditional comprehensive secondary schools. [10]

The values to which Alliance schools are expected to subscribe are:

1. To see the teacher as both friend and mentor, and to acknowledge the importance of relationships for the development of the whole person.

2. To develop a curriculum that can be tailored to the needs of the individual child.
3. To see the parents and children as partners in the process of education.
4. To undertake to develop the whole person, the moral, spiritual, creative and emotional aspects as well as the intellectual and physical, both through the curriculum and through the ethos of the school.

It will be seen that these two approaches have a lot in common, though some of the Coalition's principles challenge assumptions that we make on this side of the Atlantic. The first might seem to be one of these, though in his paper Professor David Hargreaves backs a hypothesis that schools that specialise or have a distinctive philosophy 'are more likely to be effective and to promote excellence'. The Germans and French, for instance, offer technical and vocational courses, with high intellectual content, from 12-14 onwards. (Principle 1 of the Nine.)

At the Hartland Small School we restricted the number of GCSEs that can be taken so that a package of five, maths, science, English, art and humanities, may be achieved by all. English literature and French are optional extras. The results have been very satisfactory and the school has come high in the area league table (Principles 2 & 3). A high proportion of coursework in GCSE subjects, and the Graded Assessment in Maths project - personalised learning - also contributed to success and a sense of achievement. The reduction of the coursework element has been a bitter blow (Principles 4 & 5). The Exhibition would be a natural and welcome development if it could be made acceptable to employers and further education establishments.

I, personally, would favour a radical approach to testing. We have had two pupils sit the Oxford entrance exam. I believe all universities should devise their own selection criteria and not base their decisions on 'A' levels, a poor means of assessing suitability for a university course. I would give candidates half-a-day of lectures, a seminar and some resource material and get them to write an essay on the second day. I would then know if they could benefit from what we had to offer. Employers, too, should, as some already do, set their own selection procedures and abandon any fixed ties with public exams. 'A' levels and GCSEs could then be replaced by a combination of coursework and Exhibition (Principle 6).

'Parents as partners' has always been a motto of the Small School and discipline has been achieved through an emphasis on self-discipline and trust (Principle 7). I taught English, humanities, RE and music to GCSE, as well as drama and building, and other teachers cover an equally broad range. We also have seen ourselves as counsellors, social workers, uncles and aunts. (Principle 8). We also accepted principle 9, though we took 15% to be the extra cost of a small school, which is the proportion the Danish government asks parents to find in their small schools.

The Hartland Small School did not base itself on these Sizer principles but has come to them quite independently. Our reference point was Denmark, where state-funded small schools have been part of the scene for many, many years. In Holland and some German states, too, parent-run schools get government money.

Where do third sector schools stand in England and Wales?

Where do new third sector schools stand in this country? There is a distinction to be made between those schools that would like government funding and those that wish to remain independent of the system. The latter includes schools such as Sands and Summerhill, some new Christian, some Moslem and some Jewish schools. Among the former are schools such as the Small Schools in Hartland, Bath, Ticknell and Goole, that subscribe to the values of Human Scale Education, the Steiner/Waldorf schools, many new Christian, Moslem, Jewish and Seventh Day Adventist schools. These we are building into a Third Sector Alliance. The criteria drawn up by a working group for schools wanting to join the Alliance are as follows:

1. The school is open to all irrespective of colour, creed, intellectual ability, social class or economic status.

2. The school is a day-school with a defined local catchment area.

3. The school is parent/community/teacher run.

4. No individual or group stands to gain financially from the school except in terms of salaries for teaching and administrative staff.

5. The school is registered with the DfE and as a charity.

6. Though a school may have a particular philosophical, religious or spiritual ethos it does not seek to convert those attending the school who do not subscribe to that particular philosophy or faith except through example.

7. The school teaches a broad and balanced curriculum such as the National Curriculum which enables pupils to pass on to the next stage of schooling without disadvantage, including, where relevant, higher education, or employment.

Those who are worried about having such bedfellows might like to consider the following points:

1. It is parents who, according to the 1944 Education Act, are responsible for the education of their children. They should be able to choose a school that has an ethos that reflects their own convictions and values.

2. No schools are value-free and most reflect contemporary materialist values. Some have rules that make life difficult for members of ethnic minorities. Dress codes may be inappropriate. Some require Muslim girls to participate with boys in PE and they are asked to wear kit that to them is immodest. It is difficult for Muslim teenage girls to be free, in terms of behaviour and dress, in a school that has men in it.

3. Schools that have been started for Muslim girls are not seedbeds of reaction. The girls have as role-models well-educated, successful Moslem women. In fact, such schools are likely to be seen as a threat by narrow fundamentalists within the community.

4. Similarly, many Christian schools have not been started so as to promote biblical literalism and the teaching of Creationism

instead of evolution. Their founders are more likely to be influenced by a desire to see their children educated in an ethos of love and respect for each other and for the environment, together with a healthy scepticism about the materialist values of consumption and consumerism. Even those that are committed to the Creationist explanation understand the need to teach the hypothesis of evolution as well.

5. It needs to be remembered that all the major faiths are committed to the pursuit of truth. This does not guarantee that all schools will be equally liberal in their approach but it is a feature that acceptance and openness ought to encourage.

The agreed criteria and values make it relatively easy to distinguish between those schools which it is reasonable to ask the government to support and those who, because they are unwilling to answer to anyone but themselves, put themselves beyond the pale. This will make it much easier to meet a frequent objection: If we give you funding, where will it stop? Any precedent will only be for a clearly defined group of schools. Without such agreed criteria the government is always going to use the precedent argument for refusing applications. At present all the government sees of new, 'Third Sector', schools is individual applications. They do not seem aware of the breadth of parental concern that this represents.

A school considering joining the Alliance will naturally have to take account of the conditions attached, and this could make them consider issues to which they may not have given due attention. It could even be a means of persuading some to change their policy.

Change requires political will. When the Hartland Small School first pursued state funding it was told by the Department to apply for voluntary aided status. When Lord Young of Dartington put the case for new schools in a debate in the House of Lords on the Education Reform Bill in 1988, Baroness Hooper, replying for the Government, said: ... 'it is open to any minority group with a need for education of a particular kind to apply for voluntary aided status.' What she did not say was that no school has been given voluntary aided status since 1944, nor have any since 1988. There are approximately 5,000 Church of England, 2,000 Roman Catholic and 20 Jewish voluntary aided schools receiving 100% of their running costs from the government. It does not seem unreasonable for other religious groups to want to muscle in on the action. Club members are not terribly interested in enlarging it, however:

I wrote to all the bishops with seats in the House of Lords. My own bishop, Exeter, was sympathetic but unhopeful. The Bishop of Peterborough was 'entirely happy' that Moslem schools should receive state funding so long as they are subject to the same sorts of rule that govern admission and administration to C of E schools. Only one other Bishop has, to my knowledge, been as forthright and that was the RC Bishop of Leeds, the Rt. Rev. David Konstant, who told a North of England Education Conference that 'The experience of my own community (which had been a persecuted minority) is that having our own school within the state system helped us to move out of our initial isolation, so as to become more confident and self-assured. The effect of separate schools for us has been integration not divisiveness. Despite the propaganda I do not accept that separate schools in Northern Ireland have either promoted or fuelled the long existing divisions in that torn country.' This is a view (not necessarily the Northern Ireland bit) shared by the Chief Rabbi, Jonathan Sachs, and expressed in his Reith Lectures.

A representative voice of the opposition is that of the Bishop of Gloucester, who asked to be quoted in full. 'I do not claim to be an expert on educational matters, but I am not yet persuaded in favour of the kind of liberation which would enable almost any group of people who could meet the necessary educational criteria to run their own school with funds provided by the State. I have no doubt that this would be beneficial to schools such as your own, and for that matter to at least some Muslim schools. But the practical inability to draw the line anywhere in particular would, I believe, let into the system a good number of undesirable outfits which would not benefit the children involved and impoverish the community of much needed talent. The historical position of the Church of England I see as being a rather different question, and though it is embarrassing to be defending our own somewhat privileged position, I believe the present system of Church Aided Schools is only defensible because in the main they operate as bona fide Community Schools or Neighbourhood Schools. 'I fear you will find this a disappointing response but it comes with good wishes to you and your school nonetheless.'

It doesn't really need me to underline the flaws in the argument, does it? Peter de la Cour, describing the Danish alternative school system, funded by the government since 1851, has written, 'A new school simply informs the ministry of its existence and it is then entitled to claim the state subsidy with a minimum of fuss. The basic idea is the very democratic one that consumers in the education market should have the benefit of doubt as to what constitutes a reasonable way of running a school.' We may never get it so easy here. A way forward might be the following new approach to GMS being proposed by the Alliance and already presented to the Funding Agency, the DfE and the Labour party. (To the latter, Alliance schools would be Foundation schools.)

Grant Maintained Status

The preparation of a statement of case for GM status which a school has to make is presently very time and resource consuming, as Oak Hill, one of only three grass roots initiatives that have applied, has discovered. This is, in large part, because of the requirement to make projections and demonstrate use/demand and, on the basis of these, estimate revenue and capital costs. The work involved is out of all proportion to the size of many schools that might apply, and requires skills and a time commitment which they do not possess and cannot afford. We propose a new approach for parent-run schools in the reluctant private sector:

1. A group wishing to opt in to GMS must first start their school.

2. At the end of the first year they will, if they satisfy the requirements, receive a DfE number:

3. During the second or later years they may apply to the DfE to be funded for a further three years on a per capita rate based on that of the nearest state primary or comprehensive school or on the going rate for GM schools.

4. Funding will be granted only for running and not for capital costs.

5. During the three-year period the school will be visited regularly to ensure that it is being run responsibly.

6. Towards the end of its third funded year it will receive a full inspection and a decision on the granting of GMS made on the basis of criteria to be developed.

7. If GM status is refused, funding for a further year will be negotiated so as to ensure the school closes itself in an orderly and responsible way or develops alternative sources of funding.

This proposal,

- ensures the seriousness and determination of the founders;
- allows them to show what they can do with reasonable resources;
- does not require the government to commit itself to capital expenditure during the trial period;
- will not cost the government more to educate these children than for them to be in the local state school;
- makes it possible to trial the Danish system;
- allows parents the possibility of real choice of school and meaningful involvement in its running;
- introduces into the system a flexibility that will enable the system to cope more effectively with fluctuations in pupil numbers.

We believe these proposals to be eminently reasonable. This sort of approach might go a long way to defusing the prejudice and associated anger that talk of minority schools arouses. Instead of arguing about possible outcomes we would be able to examine, and make an informed decision on, real, running schools.

Where might this lead? A failing comprehensive, say in inner Birmingham, would be closed, as recommended by Sir Tim Lankester: But instead of being reopened as the same-again-with-a-new-head-and-name it would become a campus. Within the building we might find an autonomous Muslim girls school, an autonomous Christian school, a school with a music speciality, a school with a technical emphasis and perhaps a primary school or a teacher centre. Each would have its own physical space and would share gyms, halls, playgrounds etc. By staggering starting and play times there would be a more civilised movement of bodies through the premises. Other advantages you can work out for yourself.

There would, of course, be a setting up cost, and autonomous units would be marginally more expensive to run. This, however, would be a small price to pay for the advantages to individuals and society of turning a failing school into a campus of success.

It should be clear from this hypothetical example that Alliance schools could have an important affect on improving the state sector where it is most vulnerable. So our proposals are not about pandering to the sensitivities of a handful of neurotic parents but of introducing fundamental changes that could have far-reaching consequences to what is presently the state sector.

The Curriculum

One sticking point would seem to be the curriculum. Where, for instance, do Steiner and Muslim schools stand with regard to the National Curriculum? Some schools will be agreeable to teaching the National Curriculum - some already are. Steiner schools will not abandon their own tried and tested curriculum. This need not exclude them.

'The solution to the problem of the national curriculum lies in the little-noticed Sections 16 and 17 of the 1988 Education Reform Act. Section 16 permits schools to apply to the Secretary of State to opt out of the National Curriculum, in part or in whole. Section 17 allows the Secretary of State to authorise any departure from the National Curriculum, by regulation.' [11]

Section 16 (1) of the 1988 Education Reform Act specifies that the purpose for which the Secretary of State may grant exemption, in whole or in part, is to enable development work or experiments to be carried out. All that is required in the case of a grant-maintained, aided or special agreement school, is an application by the governing body.

James Tooley draws attention to the reason given by Mrs Angela Rumbold, Minister of State at the DES, for drafting what became Section 16. It was to ensure that 'desirable curriculum development work should not be hampered or curtailed by the national curriculum', which, she stressed, was not 'set in stone'. He also points out that Sir Ron Dearing recommended in December 1993 that schools apply under Section 16 for permission to teach the National Curriculum Council's new technology curriculum on an experimental basis, which implies that they opt out of the National Curriculum regulations for technology.

The Secretary of State certainly has the power to accept alternative curricula. Whether he uses it is, of course, another matter:

But what about other people's power? The question you may be asking is, What can I do to improve schooling? Here are a few suggestions.

What can parents do?

Parents need to know what is going on in their children's schools and why. According to the 1944 Education Act, they are responsible for the education of their children. The government runs schools on their behalf. If you are a parent do not hesitate to ask your MP, your Chief Education Officer, your chairman of governors, your head teacher, your child's form teacher/tutor and subject teachers to explain and justify whatever it is they are doing. They are all answerable to you.

In many Japanese schools parents have a room of their own. Work with other parents to get a base in the school where you can meet and swap stories. Become well-informed about curriculum content and teaching approaches.

Supplement what goes on in school with outings to museums, exhibitions, art galleries, concerts, the theatre and the cinema. If you have a video, get some good tapes. Buy books. Let your children see you reading, and enjoying it. Do not let your own education slip.

Give your children quality time. Listen to younger children read. Find out what their homework is, ensure that they have a quiet time and space, and help them where possible. If you do not understand the maths, for instance, ask the school to run an evening class for parents. Look to see how homework has been received. Complain if the teacher does not make constructive comments on the work. (These are more useful than marks.) Invite the class teacher or tutor to visit you at home.

If there are crises in the home, such as an impending divorce or a serious illness, for instance, tell the school.

If your school really is appalling, think about getting together with other parents to start a new one. HSE can help you with this. It can also supply speakers to address particular educational issues. It will be immediately apparent that these remarks are addressed to middle class parents, that is, the ones who are likely to be reading this book. You are probably already doing most of the things listed above, unless you are an overworked education officer or a depressed head. What of the parents who would never touch a book like this? The intention behind comprehensive schools was that they should be socially mixed, the stronger parents making demands that would meet the needs of the children of the weaker: That is why many socialists do not like seeing an élite creamed off into independent schools.

I wish I could suggest a simple solution to the problem of compensating for the shortcomings of the home - I put it this way because sometimes the culturally rich live in emotional poverty; it is not a matter of status or class or intelligence - because school can only ever offer half an education. Are our divisions self-perpetuating? Are we the victims of our genes?

What can teachers do?

Trust your pupils and seek the co-operation of their parents; they are your partners in the education process. Visit the home and get to know the whole person of the pupil. Make yourself available. Let pupils and parents have your phone number so you can answer homework and other queries. Organise outings for small groups outside school time.

To teach well you need to be fit. Identify whatever in your work situation is a source of stress, put it in writing and send it to your head teacher: If this is too direct for you, then go through your health and safety officer or your union representative. Your employer is required to take steps to ensure that the problem does not get any worse.

You are the model: who you are is more important than what you teach. Do you embody all the qualities you look for in your pupils?

Am you broadening your interests, sharpening up your skills and trying to live honestly?

Relax. Discover silence and carry it with you into the classroom.

Try and reduce the number of pupils you see in a week by asking the head if you can teach two subjects to the same classes. (Essential Schools recommended maximum: 80 pupils per week. Norm: 160 per day.)

Try and teach individuals rather than classes.

Give up textbooks and destroy worksheets.

Get to know your colleagues, their strengths and weaknesses, and give support where you can.

Find ways of making school a happy experience for pupils.

If you are in a large school, start discussions with your colleagues about breaking it down into small, autonomous units.

If the pressure gets too much, you could just leave, but make sure that your experience is recorded. Send a copy to HSE. Then you might help parents start their own school.

What can pupils do?

Do not accept boring or badly taught lessons, though you must develop the skill of putting your point politely. Give positive feedback to teachers, too. They need to know how they are doing and your response could be more important to them than that of inspectors.

Use your parents, but try not to get impatient with them if they do not understand the way you do things. They, too, are capable of learning. In trying to teach them you may be facing difficulties that your own teachers have to cope with.

Take responsibility for your own education. If school does not provide you with all you need, find other resources: people, clubs, books etc.

Do not allow tests and exams to dominate your life. If you are clever, all your teachers will want you to sit their subject. Resist their entreaties. You need five GCSEs, including English and maths, and possibly science and a language, for university entrance. I would make eight a maximum. Study other subjects for enlightenment and pleasure.

Ask for a share in decision making in the life of the school. Suggest ways of making it a happier place.

Develop an independent line: do not just follow the crowd. Let them follow you.

Take responsibility for the behaviour of the group, especially when no teacher is present. There is always a reason for bad behaviour: Find out what it is. Is there anything you can do about it?

What can politicians do?

Realise your limitations. Education used to have a low profile, politically, as it still does in France and Germany, because ministers sought for consensus. Do not try and control what goes on in schools but content yourself with supplying the tools needed to do the job.

Do not assume that a replication of your own education will solve all our problems. See diversity as a strength, not a weakness, and encourage it.

Encourage debate.

Support innovative projects such as parent-run schools so that they may deliver a better education. Encourage them to try new approaches to teaching and to the curriculum. Pay for proper monitoring and evaluation so we may all learn from their experience.

Learn about the approach to education of other countries, but treat their systems with caution. It may not be possible to match Japanese maths results without becoming more Japanese in our thinking.

Challenge all received wisdom, in particular, the belief that large schools offer a better education than small schools, that subject specialists are more desirable than generalists, that tests and exams give a rounded assessment of pupils' abilities and that educational research can tell you anything useful that common sense cannot.

What can educationists do?

Tell the truth about the limitations of research.

Identify and disseminate good practice.

Speak and act in the interests of the child, not the teacher, the administrator or the university department, and recommend policies that can benefit everyone, not merely an 'acceptable' percentage of the school population.

Spend time in the classroom.

Use language that parents can easily understand.

Make life difficult for yourself by refusing to accept the simple solutions that grow out of topdown thinking.

If all these people did all these things the prospects for our children might be considerably brighter: I will leave you with some words of Robin Pedley, promoter of the comprehensive school: *Freedom in education is a first requirement for the establishment and maintenance of a free society. It must be preserved. This means, however: more than an absence of controls; it means having the wherewithal to live freely: money.* [12]

References

1. Hughill, B. and Narayan, N. *Must Try Harder,* in Observer article (5.11.95) quoting figures supplied by the National Institute of Economic and Social Research.

2. McPake, J. and Powney, J. (1995) *A Mirror to Ourselves? The Educational Experience of Japanese Children at School in the UK.* Scottish Council for Research in Education.

3. Archambault, D. (1967) Preface to *Tolstoy on Education.* The University of Chicago Press.

4. Chubb, J. and Moe, T. Article in the *Sunday Times* (9.2.92).

5. Ancess, J. (1995) *Coming Down the Home Stretch: Transforming a Comprehensive High School into an Educational Campus.* NCREST, University of Columbia, NY.

6. Darling-Hammond, L., Ancess, J., McGregor, K., and Zuckerman, D. (1995). *The Coalition Campus Schools Project: Inching Toward Systematic Change in New York City.* NCREST, University of Columbia, NY.

7. Ancess, J. (1995) *An Inquiry High School: Learner-Centered Accountability at the Urban Academy.* NCREST, University of Columbia, NY

8. From an ACS handbook. Cf. also Lehman, D. *Building Community in an Alternative Secondary School in Public Schools that Work,* edited by Gregory A. Smith.

9. Sizer, T. *Diverse Practice, Shared Ideas: the Essential School.* In *Organizing for Learning: Toward the 21st Century,* edited by Herbert J. Walberg and John J. Lane. National Association of Secondary School Principals (1989).

10. The Principles may be found in (8) and on almost everything published by the Coalition of Essential Schools, Brown University. The Coalition of Campus Schools Project's adapted version can be found as an appendix to (5).

11. Tooley, J. (1995) *Denationalizing the Curriculum: From Bureaucratic Monolith to Safety-Net* .

12. Pedley, R. (1963,4,6) *The Comprehensive School.* Penguin.

'Opting in' under the 1993 Education Act: A case study of Oak Hill School, Bristol

Ruth Deakin

The 1993 Education Act enables independent schools to 'opt-in' to Grant Maintained Status and voluntary bodies to promote such schools and therefore to obtain public funding - in theory if not in practice. This case study examines some of the issues raised by the opportunity to create new schools, and for independent schools to 'opt in'. I will use examples from one particular school, Oak Hill School in Bristol, and from the process of lobbying with which the School was involved on behalf of a number of new alternative and independent schools for access to public funding. Whilst this is a specific case study, the issues outlined here are common to all schools wishing to 'opt in' .

I will suggest that this new legislative opportunity, whilst it furthers the government's own Grant Maintained Policy, also gives unprecedented opportunities for communities to be empowered to engage in the task of education. It potentially increases the range of schools available for parents to choose between, and will enable 'bottom up' initiatives in education to flourish and contribute to the state system of provision. In a pluralist, multicultural society it is important that the state, either local or central, does not impose its own ideology on schools, but enables a variety of types of schools to exist within a common framework. That common framework in Britain at present is extensive, and statutory requirements on admissions, curriculum, and structure will ensure that only those schools which can genuinely be of benefit to the wider community will be able to pursue this route.

Oak Hill School: a short history

Oak Hill School opened as an independent school in 1984 with a junior and infant department in premises owned by an evangelical Christian church in the north of Bristol. It was started by a community of parents and teachers who were dissatisfied with the values and standards of behaviour observed in some local state schools. There was also a desire to explore and develop an educational philosophy and practice which was shaped by the beliefs and values of the Christian faith. Initially the school was directly linked through its governing body with a particular church, although since 1989 it has been independently constituted as an educational charity.

In 1986 the school moved to new premises which were purchased as a result of parents donating the money (£77,500) with the support of local churches. The pupil roll soon rose to around 80 and as an adequate number reached the end of the primary school age a decision was taken to move into the secondary phase of education, and in 1989 the senior department moved to new rented premises. In 1994 the first small cohort of pupils took their GCSEs achieving results which astounded supporters and critics alike - nearly 30% of all papers marked were either A or A starred. The pupils did particularly well in the core subjects of the National Curriculum.

Parental involvement in the school is high - parent helpers in the classrooms, in extra curricular activities, in fundraising, in administration and in development work. Many of the teachers are also parents of children at the school.

Parents are asked to contribute 10% of their income to the school, and in addition to pay a small capitation fee. However a large proportion of parents fall within a medium to low income bracket. As a consequence some families contribute only the capitation fee, since the school has always had a policy of not excluding families who cannot afford to contribute the full 10%. The school has an open admissions policy, admitting pupils of all abilities and attracting a significant minority of families with social and economic needs. In addition teachers have been prepared to work for unusually low remuneration. Despite enormous commitment, the senior school proved financially unsustainable and closed down in 1994, with the bulk of students transferring to a Voluntary Aided Church School elsewhere in the city.

At the same time the school succeeded in becoming the first independent school to apply to the newly created Funding Agency for Schools to become Grant Maintained and to relocate and expand and develop the school to serve a new community in the north of the city.

The 'Christian Schools Movement'

Oak Hill is just one example of what has been described as the phenomenon of the Christian schools movement in England and Wales. While historically the Churches have always been involved in education, indeed today over 7,000 of state schools are Voluntary Aided or Voluntary Controlled Church Schools, the last ten years has seen a resurgence of community led initiatives to establish new Christian schools. Parallel to this there has been a smaller growth in schools of other faiths, particularly Islam, and schools which subscribe to different educational approaches, such as the 'Human Scale Education Movement', and Steiner schools.

These schools together form what Geoffrey Walford describes as the 'reluctant private sector' - they are independent because at the time of opening they did not perceive the state system to be providing what their parents wanted, rather than because they have an ideological commitment to private education. Furthermore they serve families from all socio-economic backgrounds.

Over 90 new Christian schools of this type have been established during the eighties and the early nineties. The majority of them were established by local groups of parents and church leaders, independently of one another, and in response to both negative and positive stimuli. They are enormously diverse in terms of their sponsoring groups, theological orientation, and in the development of their educational theory and practice. McKenzie's research into thirty nine of these schools identifies both positive and negative stimuli which account for their growth. She summarises these as a response to perceived dominant educational ideologies which are essentially secular, and therefore marginalise a Christian world view, and as a positive attempt to develop educational theory and practice which is shaped by a Judeo-

Christian perspective on life, thus making a positive Christian contribution to a healthier society. (McKenzie 1994)

The campaign for public funding

Since all of the schools have generally not selected families on the grounds of the parents' ability to pay realistically for private education, the issue of access to public funding has been one which has been significant for the new Christian schools, and other schools within the 'reluctant private sector'. The profound changes in the education service during this time, with an emphasis on parental choice, diversity, and self management of schools has provided momentous opportunities for the schools to organise themselves and to lobby for the access to public funding which is now enshrined on the statute books in the 1993 Act. In the presence of enormous 'top down' policy making by the Conservative government, this is a fascinating 'bottom up' initiative.

This process of lobbying has resulted in a substantial opportunity for communities of all sorts to be empowered to engage in the provision of education at a level which is unprecedented in England and Wales during this century. It is, I suggest, an unintended outcome of Conservative policy which sought to promote parental choice through the introduction of market forces into education. It is an outcome which fits well with the neo-liberal conservatives' belief in individual liberty and a free market. The neo-conservative wing of the Tory party are sympathetic to the emphasis on Christian virtues and morals, but they have much greater problems when it comes to equal treatment for schools of all faiths and philosophies. The debates in the Lords over the various legislative initiatives which culminated in the 'opting in' clauses of the 1993 Education Act are evidence of how the debate provoked enormous controversy and was entirely unpredictable along party lines, with no consensus evident in any one political party.

'Opting in' - how to do it

Oak Hill School has been at the forefront of schools wishing to pursue 'opting-in'. In October 1994 Oak Hill Trust made application to the Secretary of State under Section 49 of the 1993 Education Act to establish a new GM school in Bristol. The key point about section 49 is that the promoter of the proposal is a voluntary body, not a Local Education Authority or government quango. The application process is described in a DFE (now DFEE) circular (number 23/94) entitled *'The Supply of School Places'* and a document called *'Guidance to Promoters on establishing new Grant Maintained Schools'*.

Proposals become formal when they are 'published', literally in a newspaper, and the published proposals together with a Statement of Case constitute the application. Getting to this point is a huge task and in Oak Hill's case has entailed much research, ingenuity, negotiation, some compromise and enormous tenacity especially given that the Funding Agency for Schools (FAS), the 'quango' with responsibility for planning new GM schools, has only just (in October 1995) 18 months after its establishment, produced formal guidelines for potential promoters.

The application process begins with informal consultation with the FAS who are interested in two broad aspects of Section 49 proposals: the 'idea' and 'implementability'. The idea is constituted of issues like the character, the need for and the financial viability of the school. The implementability boils down to the practical issues such as capital costs, whether the promoter can fund at least 15% of these costs, the suitability of premises, acquisition of land required, and so on. The principal concerns of the FAS officers in Oak Hill's experience were to do with capital costs, whether the school would attract enough pupils, whether the promoting body can deliver its contribution to capital costs and whether land required was obtainable. The FAS officers offer their view on the likelihood of the Agency's support or opposition to the proposals at an early stage.

Although not required, it is advisable to informally consult the DFEE also since the published proposals must be technically correct in terms of, for example, the category of the school, the details of the governing body, and the school location. Also the proposal must include details of admission arrangements and these arrangements must follow DFEE guidelines and directives. If flawed there are potential grounds for objection to or rejection of the proposals on technical grounds alone.

The next stage is formal consultation with a lengthy list of bodies which includes the FAS, the LEA, the governing body of each of the local schools, parents in the area, parents and teachers of an existing independent school and other interested bodies, and is laid down in circular 23/94. In the Oak Hill case there were about 40 different bodies and groups to consult. The content of the consultation should include the proposals in draft form together with supporting documents such as a summary statement of case. Care must be taken over the time allowed for response to the consultation, ideally 8 weeks excluding school holiday periods (when educationalists may not be available!). The consultation documents and responses received must be submitted to the Secretary of State. The most critical response is that of the FAS and in Oak Hill's case their formal response came only after three months.

The Statement of Case

The bulk of work involved in making an application to 'opt-in' however lies in the preparation of a detailed statement of case, which sets out the reasons why the promoters believe the Secretary of State should support their proposals. There is a pro-forma available from the DFEE although this document does not offer suggestions for strengthening the case - this is up to the ingenuity and effort of the promoter's responsible person. Potentially the research and preparation could be a full-time job for 3-6 months particularly if the relevant LEA is unwilling to co-operate in supplying required data. The pro-forma has 18 sections including the constitution of the promoting body itself, the need for school, staffing and management arrangements, curriculum structure, exam results and what happens if the application is unsuccessful. The central issues are those dealing with pupil numbers and school places in the area and demand for the proposed school.

Bottoms on seats

Detailed pupil projection data, which has to cover a 3 year period, can only be obtained from the LEA and in most areas the LEA is not obliged to provide this information. The LEA in Oak Hill's case is Avon which refused to provide this information. It can be gleaned from Education Committee reports though these may be inadequate. Sympathetic councillors may be able to help or as a last resort the DFEE or FAS may have some relevant data or be able to request the data from the LEA on the promoter's behalf.

The purpose of this data is to establish whether there is a 'basic need' case which is related to the presence or absence of surplus places compared with projected pupil numbers in the area. Generally, schools wishing to 'opt-in' will find it difficult to gain the support of the FAS if there are unfilled (surplus) relevant school places in the area (a 2 mile radius of a proposed primary school and a 3 mile radius if secondary) especially if the number of unfilled places is greater than 10% of the total capacity in the area. In most instances however, the case for 'opting-in' will be based not on 'basic-need' but on 'parental demand'. Parental demand is, simply, parental preference for a particular school or type of school. The statement of case would have to offer sufficient evidence that pupils will fill the proposed school. Suitable evidence is a track record of appropriate pupil numbers at an existing school or statements of intent signed by prospective parents in sufficient numbers to demonstrate sustained demand in the case of a brand new school. *There is currently no formal guidance as to what constitutes sufficient numbers or what constitutes evidence of parental demand.* The FAS' head of planning suggested to Oak Hill that 2 statements of intent for each place created would be necessary. This is remarkable given that historically new Roman Catholic and Anglican schools provide baptismal certificates on a one-for-one basis.

It appears that a case made on a parental demand basis and involving substantial capital costs is less likely to gain the support of the FAS than one which does not. In Oak Hill's case the FAS were willing to support a proposal for a primary school requiring minimal capital, but for which even the Oak Hill team considered there was inadequate evidence of parental demand. The FAS were unwilling to support a primary and secondary proposal with substantial evidence of demand but with substantial capital costs. One might infer that the notion of 'implementability' in this respect is strategically more important to the FAS than the 'idea' of a proposed new school.

Strengthening the case

Specialist consultant reports may strengthen the Statement of Case. For example: suitability of premises, calculation of pupil capacity and proper estimates of any building costs; legal issues concerning the trust deed of an existing school and staff contracts; and independent assessment of the educational standards of an existing school. These probably require expert advice and can be expensive to obtain but nevertheless do demonstrate the seriousness and professionalism of the promoters.

With the first application of its kind Oak Hill's team have found that while FAS and DFEE officers and ministers are willing to discuss the various aspects of the process and case before and after publication of proposals nevertheless these are statutory bodies. Cautious and bureaucratic views of issues of 'implementability' seem to be all important, however sound the 'idea'. This tends to create the impression that the officials are only interested in the problems and that one hurdle after another is raised with either no or vague suggestions for overcoming these.There is therefore a need for an expert support service for potential promoters which can, at reasonable cost, provide good advice in a proactive manner in order to present the strongest case possible. Such a service is available through the Grant Maintained Schools Trust for maintained schools wishing to 'opt-out'. It should be available for voluntary bodies wishing to 'opt-in'.

Publishing the Proposals

The proposals in their final form, probably comprising 4 or 5 A4 pages of text then have to be published in a manner prescribed including a public notice in a newspaper. Copies are submitted to the Secretary of State along with the Statement of Case. This is followed by a two month 'statutory objection period' in which certain bodies like the FAS, the LEA, other schools and any group of 10 electors can formally object to the proposals, directly to the Secretary of State. If the LEA is opposed to the proposals media coverage can become substantial and unpleasant, but the promoter can request the DFEE to give sight of any objections submitted and then offer some counter arguments.

Opposition from the educational establishment

The Grant Maintained Status policy has always been highly contested since it is essentially moving power away from Local Education Authorities and creating a system where there is no accountability structure between individual governing bodies and central government. Many schools which have sought to 'opt out' have encountered fierce and unpleasant opposition and it has become apparent that 'opting in' is going to provoke the same controversy. During the consultation period in Oak Hill School's case, the response from the Avon Director of Education to the proposals was that 'the best form of amendment is abandonment' (letter to Oak Hill School, May 1994). Furthermore the opposition to the proposals has been fuelled by officers of the Local Education Authority, and their contribution to the local debate has been described as 'misleading' by a minister of state in the Department for Education (letter to Oak Hill School from DfE 11/8/94). Avon LEA circulated all schools (approx 450) in Avon with a report which set out a case against the proposals. Included in this argument were the alleged financial costs LEA controlled schools would lose from the revenue budget. These alleged costs were described by the Funding Agency for Schools as 'a red herring' and in fact refuted by that agency. Nevertheless, the damage was done and many maintained schools submitted formal objections to the Secretary of State (which they are entitled to do under the legislation).

The decision

The Secretary of State then considers the proposals and Statement of Case and may commission an OFSTED inspection of an existing school. A decision or determination of the proposals should follow around five months after publication, although in Oak Hill's case a determination took almost exactly 12 months. The uncertainty created by this delay greatly hindered normal planning, especially over staffing matters and highlights the need for a more proactive and flexible approach on the part of the FAS and DFEE.

Key controversies

I will endeavour to outline some of the key issues related to 'opting in' which have formed the heart of the controversy in Oak Hill School's case, and will seek to present the reasons why the school is prepared to persist in the face of such fierce opposition and at such a high cost, both in human and financial terms.

Religious Schools and Sectarianism

One of the most enlightening aspects of the lobbying for public funding which the Christian Schools Campaign (subsequently subsumed within Christian Action Research and Education (CARE)) undertook alongside groups representing schools of other faiths and philosophies, was the profound antipathy from some which exists towards religious schools, and the tenacity with which people cling to the idea that schools can somehow be 'value neutral'. To create new publicly funded religious schools would be to foster an intolerant, divided and sectarian society. Why not include all children in 'common' schools and treat all faiths equally within it?

The claim that religious schools foster intolerance is an empirical claim which is not supported by evidence. In fact there is a growing body of research which indicates that religious schools need not and do not foster intolerance (Greely and Rossi 1966 pp 116, 130, 136, Greer and McElhinney 1984, 1985, Greer 1985, Hornsby-Smith 1978).

Historical and comparative precedents

The involvement of religious communities in the task of schooling is not a new concept in the UK. Indeed nearly one third of British schools are Voluntary Aided or Controlled church schools. To be truly equitable either the dual system should be abolished, as was suggested in the Swann Report (1985, p.498,520,774), or it should be extended to include the new religious and philosophical communities which are characteristic of contemporary British society. It is technically possible under the 1980 Education Act for new Voluntary Aided Schools to be established, but this requires the support of the Local Education Authority. Persistent attempts by some of these schools to enter the state funded sector by this route have been unsuccessful, usually due to the lack of support from the LEA. In one widely publicised case, that of Islamia Primary School in London, it was finally turned down by the Secretary of State even though it had gained the support of the Local Education Authority. Thus the opportunities presented in the 1993 Education Act present the only realistic route into public funding for these schools.

Funding for religious and alternative schools is not a new concept in other Western education systems either, and indeed in some Eastern European countries governments are funding new religious schools following the breakdown of communism. Whilst the use of international policy borrowing should be undertaken with care, it is clear that the central organising idea - that the state does not have the right to impose a particular educational ideology on all schools - is far from unusual, and shapes educational provision in countries as disparate as the Netherlands, Denmark, Germany, France, Australia, Canada, Romania and Hungary. The 1944 Education Act states that 'it is the duty of every Local Education Authority to secure that there shall be for their area sufficient schools' ...which shall be 'suitable to the requirements' of pupils and... 'sufficient in number, character and equipment' (p5). Attention has been given since 1944 to sufficiency and suitability in terms of numbers, but perhaps less in terms of character, and the requirements of pupils and their parents especially in terms of their beliefs and values.

Beliefs and values shape all schools

A growing body of research indicates that all observable educational practice is grounded in educational ideas and assumptions. These ideas, assumptions and beliefs are those about children, those about society and those about knowledge. Educational ideas, assumptions and beliefs form a part of an individual's wider belief system, or worldview, which in turn is profoundly influenced by cultural and communal belief systems. Communal belief systems, or ideologies are powerful determinants of educational practice and provision. No school therefore can be value free in its educational approach.

The importance of vision

The educational beliefs and values which are held by a school community are what should form that school's vision. A school's vision, or its goals, values and guiding principles, is a critical factor in determining the direction of the school which shapes the implementation of curricular and management policies, and contributes to the distinctiveness of the school. Ernest (1991) demonstrates in some detail how different educational beliefs promote different views of mathematics - which has been typically viewed as the paradigm of certain knowledge - and in turn these lead to often very different teaching and learning styles, schemes of work and curricular materials.

Effective leadership is intimately linked by research to effective schools - effective in terms of teaching and learning - and whilst the search for laws of educational leadership is problematic, a clear and coherent educational vision which is widely shared by the school community is undoubtedly a very significant factor (Green 1992, Caldwell and Spinks 1992, Hodgkinson 1992, Sergiovanni 1983, West 1993, Nias 1989, Angus 1989). The movement towards school autonomy, or self management, underlines the importance of school based leadership. Furthermore, research on school effectiveness indicates that the active support of the parent community in the school is another important factor in determining effectiveness. Shared vision and values is evidently a substantial component in the task of fostering a sense of community and active participation with parents in the process of education. A strong and shared educational vision is one of the distinctive features of the schools within the reluctant private sector.

Whose vision of education should the school be serving?

In a pluralist, multicultural society where a variety of belief systems can be seen to be competing for expression in society and in schools, the ethics of educational leadership moves centre stage. A central question becomes: Whose vision of education should the school be serving?

The role of the state

The advent of a heavily prescribed national curriculum has been widely criticised and has shown that there is not a broadly held consensus about the content of the curriculum. For the government to impose a particular set of values and curriculum on all schools produces conflict and is arguably inequitable for those teachers and parents who do not share those values. It follows too that the same can apply to a Local Education Authority, which is a more local expression of government. Indeed the evidence from many Local Education Authorities with whom schools in the reluctant private sector have sought to achieve Voluntary Aided Status indicates that LEAs can be as ideologically driven by a particular vision for education as can central government, and as unwilling to listen to dissenting parents and communities (Walford 1994).

Parental choice

Whilst the policy changes in the last ten years have been designed to promote individual parental choice, there has not been a parallel increase in the variety of types of school available for individual parents to choose between. Individual parents making choices, even when they do so for reasons based on perceived quality or religious preference, will not increase the range of choices available. Within a uniform model of schooling choice is more likely to re-inforce educational hierarchies, which are linked to social class, than to improve educational opportunities or overall quality. One of the distinctive features of the new Christian schools is that they cater for families from all social and economic backgrounds, which is a central reason why they are so interested in government funding. In addition to this, those schools which are located in inner city areas admit children from a variety of ethnic groups. An example is the Icthus Primary School in South London which has 80% of its pupils from ethnic minority groups, many of whom also belong to diverse religious communities. Allowing diversity of schools to flourish, therefore, will increase real choice and will counter some of the economic and social impediments to choice which currently exist.

Empowering communities

The notion of the community as a powerful force in contemporary society is one which is challenging the individualist, rights based liberalism of recent years. This notion has developed from a view which gives fuller expression to the claims of citizenship. The communitarian position is that we cannot conceive of ourselves as independent from our aims and attachments. There are social attachments which determine the self and thus individuals are constituted by the community of which they are a part. MacIntyre (1992) argues that one understands one's life only by looking at one's actions within a 'narrative' which converges with the 'narratives' of other people, who come to be part of one's own narrative. Thus an understanding of oneself can only be attained in the context of community.

Setting up a school by definition is a communal task, the more so in the context of the reluctant private sector and the provision of the 1993 Education Act, because it does not happen as the result of bureaucratic dictat based on the technological rationality of mere numbers, and on the internal politics of the Local Education Authority. Any school by definition is a community in itself and is located in a wider community which it serves and which supports it.

How can schools be accountable to the community they serve ?

At this point an answer to the central question of whose educational vision should schools serve is to suggest that schools should be accountable to their communities and should be serving their community's interests by developing a vision of education which is owned and shared by the whole of the school community - parents, pupils, teachers and by the wider community including local business groups, churches and other interest groups.

Communities can be defined in a weak sense by history and geography, but the view of personhood which sees human beings as constitutionally interdependent, as 'persons-in-relation' (Wertsch 1989, Witheral and Pope Edwards 1991, Shweder 1982, Sampson 1989, Tappan 1991, Gilligan 1982, Noddings 1984, Norman 1993) leads to a much stronger understanding of community which includes shared beliefs, values and goals. In our highly mobile society, geographical and historical factors are less important, and individuals can form part of a variety of communities. Fowler describes, for example, the family community, where kinship constitutes the communal bond, the commercial community constituted by a communal bond of economic exchange, and the school community constituted by a bond of structured learning.

From this perspective, in a pluralist society, where differing ideologies of education co-exist, an equitable solution is to enable diversity to flourish amongst schools. A diversity of providers would facilitate diversity of governing body, of management structures and of ethos. This would enable these schools to promote a stronger, more consensually shared vision, than the present system which seeks to cater for all belief systems in a 'common' school, which often results in 'low doctrine' in terms of principles and values (Holmes 1992), in other words the lowest common denominator in terms of values, which is often little more than non-violence, tolerance and respect for the other person.

The community as a 'mediating structure'

The second major controversy surrounding the Grant Maintained Status policy is the debate between planned provision of schooling and a quasi-market, where individual schools compete for individual parents and their children. There is no reason, apart from the intransigence of the Local Education Authorities and the custom and practice of bureaucratic rationality, why new community schools cannot form part of a more open and planned provision of schooling. It is interesting to note that the Labour party, committed to abolishing Grant Maintained Schools should it come into power, is looking seriously at alternative local structures which could service all schools. (Times Educational Supplement 4/11/94)

Oak Hill School for example, has collaborated with the Town Council in the area of the proposed new school, in order to create a community school which serves the needs of a rapidly growing new town. Three nominees from the Bradley Stoke Town Council are to be appointed as Foundation Governors, and already share responsibility for the development of the project. The promoters seek to work with, rather than against existing schools and educational structures, but this is difficult with Avon Local Education Authority which refused to answer letters for five years regarding the acquisition of Voluntary Aided Status, and now refuses dialogue over the new proposals. Furthermore the proposed admissions policy of Oak Hill School includes the provision for up to 5% of pupils to be admitted where there are pressing social, or medical grounds for doing so.

Communitarianism includes methodological and normative arguments and moral and political claims which are evidently of significance to education. What most of its scholars, both radical and conservative, share is the advocacy of involvement in public life, the importance of participation in small communities, firms and clubs. They see these 'mediating structures' (mediating between the individual and the state) as safeguards against the potential totalitarianism of the state which might result from the 'politics of the common good' rather than the politics of individual rights.

The opportunity to 'opt-in' created by the 1993 Education Act offers precisely the possibility of communities being empowered to engage meaningfully in the provision of schooling. Rather than perpetuating an already inequitable school system, a problem of implementation and structure which is likely to be gradually ironed out by the process of confrontation and compromise between the key players or by the advent of another government, this legislation actually enables some key ideas - self management, parental choice, and community empowerment - to develop into a policy for provision of schooling which is likely to be more equitable in the longer term, and which is likely to avoid the marginalisation of minority communities.

The role of the state and the common framework

Critics of those who lobby for public funding for religious and alternative schools will cite fears of sectarianism and divisiveness in society as a whole. This indeed may be a possibility if the policy were taken to an extreme. However there exists a strong common framework for schools, which includes detailed statutory requirements for curriculum, admissions, health and safety, equal opportunities, constitution and government, as well as the

OFSTED requirements for school inspection. The National Curriculum, as a means of ensuring that all children receive a 'basic entitlement curriculum' is an appropriate measure for a government to create for all schools. The extent of the prescription of the National Curriculum in its present form, is felt by many schools to be onerous and inhibiting. However, even as it stands, it does not legislate for how the curriculum should be organised, nor the precise content.

Schools of all sorts can promote a narrow and restrictive form of education, and the schools within the 'reluctant private sector' are no exception. However, schools which do not wish to provide open access for all families or who see the national framework as too restrictive, will not wish to proceed to Grant Maintained Status. Nor should they.

In addition the actual process of 'opting in' as experienced by Oak Hill School in Bristol, is long, arduous and requires detailed planning, negotiating and to some extent compromising with officials from both the Department for Education and the Funding Agency for Schools.

In particular, although the Consultative Circular on the Supply of School Places (DFE September 1994) states that the Secretary of State will take into account both the need for diversity, quality and parental demand, proof of basic need, ie the absence of surplus places in the whole of a Local Education Authority area combined with the ability to sustain a proposed school demographically well into the future, are still the main criteria (letter from FAS to OHS). To sustain schools of the minimum size thought to be economically viable, requires significant support from the community and is more than likely going to require collaboration amongst communities of different types. It cannot by done by individual parents, but rather by groups of parents acting communally.

The admissions policies set by such schools have to comply with DFE requirements. In particular they have to be open, that is they cannot discriminate against pupils on the grounds of race, creed or gender.

'Bottom up' innovation

Finally, in a context where the very form and structure of schooling itself is being forced to respond to major global cultural changes and needs, new schools, which have had the opportunity to explore the processes of schooling outside of the existing state funded framework, may well be in a better position than most to function as forward looking schools which are responsive to the demands of self management and the needs of pupils who will grow up in the next century. Research into one of these schools described the school's religious ethos as 'having a very contemporary face' and described the teaching staff as 'giving the appearance of being, and wanting to be, on the cutting edge of educational theory and practice. Almost all of them were capable of sustaining an informed educational discussion, and two of the teachers had a number of articles published in academic journals' (Lambert 1993 p112). Whilst the City Technology Colleges have been expected to fulfill an innovatory role they have been criticised by proponents of choice as being essentially 'top down' initiatives (Chubb & Moe 1992). A system which allows the best of the 'bottom up' initiatives to flourish is more likely to be able to adapt to change from within, and to avoid alienation and polarisation within the teaching community.

The 'opting in' policy is in its infancy, and although enshrined on the statute books in the 1993 Education Act, the process of its implementation has yet to be fulfilled. However I have presented a case study of a particular school, which is not atypical of the types of schools and communities which are exploring the options presented by this legislation. I have suggested that all schools are informed by particular values and beliefs, and that in a pluralist society, which lacks confidence in a universalising belief system, a variety of different schools should be allowed to flourish. This will actually increase choice for parents and work against some of the potential social inequalities which may result from choice within a uniform model of schooling. I have drawn attention to the paradigm of communities as an important social structure which militates against individualism or its polar opposite, statism, and which provides a new perspective from which to view this legislation. The role of the state is important in providing a common framework which all schools have to adhere to and which protects the rights of children to equality of opportunity and a basic entitlement curriculum.

This paper was written with the assistance of Gary Prosser, Development Officer at Oak Hill School.

Opting in to Grant Maintained Status: A Post Script.

On 15 December 1995, fourteen months after the initial publication of proposals for Oak Hill School to 'opt in' to Grant Maintained Status, the Secretary of State communicated her decision to reject the proposals. The decision arrived by facsimile ten minutes before the end of the Christmas term. Thus in three minutes and one side of A4 paper the previous three years work came to an end.

The length of time taken over the decision was nearly three times that which was expected in the light of previous applications for Voluntary Aided Status. During the intervening months following the submission of the Statement of Case which accompanied the proposals there were a number of changes which occurred pertaining to the application. Most significant of these was the Local Education Authority's repeated updating of figures on the supply of school places, which by November 1995 had reached such a point that there was an arguable basic need case for a secondary school in the area, as well as a primary school. Also the promoters had continued to develop schemes with business and a proposal to use the Public Finance Initiative substantially supported the case. These changes were reported to the officials at the Department for Education and Employment regularly with a request that they were taken into account. Unusually a Minister of Education was willing to conduct a meeting with representatives of the promoting body in May of that year, and a flurry of official enquiries from the DFEE followed. At some points it was impossible to gauge which way the decision would go; the promoters knew that they had the support of significant politicians but the opposition of the officials.

The communication from the Secretary of State confirmed that the proposals would have added increased diversity and choice in the area but gave three reasons for the rejection:

1. There was 'insufficient evidence of demand for secondary places according to the usual criteria'.

2. The unwillingness of the existing Local Education Authority and the new Unitary Authority (new appointments for which were made from the top echelons of the existing LEA) to make the proposed site available and that the Secretary of State was unwilling to commence a potential compulsory purchase order on the proposed site.

3. The capital costs of the project, in the light of the first two objections, were the final reason given for the rejection.

Evaluation

The first reason given did not clarify one of the primary policy issues of the legislation - that of the weight given to parental demand over and against 'basic need', which is based purely on the LEA's projected figures of demographic changes. In a meeting with John Patten, then Secretary of State for Education, in the summer of 1994, the promoters were assured that parental demand was indeed a significant factor and that the hardest form of evidence of parental demand was signed statements of intent by prospective parents. This was subsequently accepted by the Funding Agency for Schools (FAS) with the proviso that such statements should be numbers which supported the proposed intake. The promoters produced this evidence, in numbers 3 times the proposed primary intake (which was 25 places per year group) but lower at secondary level. The number of statements for secondary places did however rise to and exceed the proposed intake (100 per year group) within 2-3 years. However when this was presented to the Funding Agency for Schools, the requirement changed to two statements of intent per place proposed for both primary and secondary.

The demographic data from the University of the West of England survey seems to have been completely discounted.

Thus 'the usual criteria' would appear to be a reference to 'basic need' which is a concept based on neither primary nor secondary legislation but simple custom and practice. This is a policy issue requiring clarification in the light of the government's espoused values of parental choice and diversity.

Both the Funding Agency and the Secretary of State relied on figures from the Local Education Authority for projected basic need even though these figures literally changed four times during the 14 months and were arguably unreliable. It is incredible that the LEA were given such power in view of the very public opposition of that LEA to our proposals.

The proposals were made in such a way that they could be implemented in a phased manner also thereby spreading capital costs over 3–4 years. The rejection of the whole proposal actually means that there remains a basic need case for primary schools in the area, despite the fact that the Secretary of State approved simultaneous proposals by the LEA for a county primary school. Basic need at primary level is such that the Secretary of State may be in breach of her statutory duty to provide sufficient school places. In addition the evidence provided by the promoters, and supported by evidence from the LEA, shows that evidence of basic need at year seven is currently unmet. The Secretary of State's unwillingness to be flexible in phasing in the proposals means that an 'on the ground' crisis in the provision of places at secondary level too will be unplanned for and unmet whilst new proposals are processed.

The implacable opposition of the LEA was a significant factor in the whole process. In public relations terms they were successful in their opposition, carrying as they do the cultural capital of 'educational orthodoxy' and authority. However its resolve to oppose the proposals was never put to the test. Had the Secretary of State decided that she was 'minded to approve the proposals' the promoters would have been in a much stronger negotiating position with local politicians who might well have supported a project which had a real chance of becoming a school as opposed to the vague promises of a new school in the new century by the LEA.

The capital costs of the project are determined by the size of the buildings and by the prevailing building cost index. However in the case of a new Voluntary Grant Maintained School the cost to the public purse would have been 15% less than that of its county school equivalent because of the promoter's contribution. Although the promoters had a substantial amount of capital to put towards the costs, their ability to raise money from other sources was limited by the uncertainty of the project prior to an approval. An indication that the Secretary of State approved of the project idea would have altered this situation significantly.

General Comments

The overall question which arises from the rejection of these proposals is one of how far is the government willing to go in its commitment to the policy of parental choice and diversity and in particular in its support of grass roots initiatives.

In the case of City Technology Colleges which are actually 'top down' initiatives the opposition of LEAs did not appear to be a problem. In Oak Hill Trust's case, it is documented that there would have been support from the FAS for a primary school application on the existing school site where, moreover, capital costs would have been minimal. However the promoters had presented no evidence of future demand at this site and knew that such an application would have been even weaker on basic need criteria. Does this belie the dominant agenda of government to minimise public spending on promoting true diversity?

No grass roots initiative in schooling is going to be straightforward in bureaucratic terms since by definition the impetus is not going to come from the usual channels of the planning departments of the LEAs or the Funding Agency. Schools wishing to 'opt in' or new voluntary bodies wishing to promote schools currently have to act as individuals, with no body to advise or support them, and with no financial support for the process. The cost of the whole process of application to Oak Hill School was substantial, both financially and in terms of management.

Policy Issues

In overall terms a number of lessons can be learned from this experience which could guide future policy making and lobbying processes.

1. The rights of parents and local communities to engage with the process of planning the supply of school places, both in terms of sufficiency and suitability need to be clarified and affirmed. It seems ridiculous that an LEA publicly opposed to GM schools in principle should be trusted to provide the 'impartial' demographic data on which proposals can stand or fall. Specifically the government needs to clarify precisely what constitutes evidence of parental demand and this needs at least appropriate secondary legislation.

2. The political polarisation which exists between the Grant Maintained sector and the County School sector is such that it obscures the real educational issues of self-management, diversity and the celebration of innovation.

3. The mode of interaction between voluntary promoters, bureaucrats and politicians need to be examined carefully. Supporting grass roots initiatives will require political commitment from any government to resource the process with information, finances and procedural support. There needs to be an adequately resourced support service to facilitate, guide and advise potential promoters, something which the DFEE and FAS cannot do because of their statutory or executive agency status and because of their unenthusiastic attitude.

4. Community initiatives will not get off the ground if the 'chicken is required before the egg', particularly in terms of capital costs and in the face of obstructive LEAs.

5. Planning for the supply of school places needs to be re-examined. In particular the evidence of basic need, the sources of such evidence, and the openness and availability of such information are factors which require public scrutiny and accountability.

References

Alexander R. (1992) *Policy and Practice in Primary Education,* London, Routledge.

Angus L. (1989) New Leadership and the Possibility of Reform, in Smyth (ed) *Critical Perspectives on Educational Leadership,* Lewes, Falmer Press.

Beck J. (1981) Education, Industry and the Needs of the Economy, *Education for Teaching* 11,2,87-106.

Bottery M. (1990) *The Morality of the School,* London, Cassell.

Bryk A.,Lee V.(1993) *Catholic Schools and the Common Good,* Cambridge, Mass., Harvard University Press.

Caldwell B.& Spinks J. (1992) *Leading the Self Managing School,* London, The Falmer Press.

Chubb J.,& Moe T. (1992) *A Lesson in School Reform from Great Britain,* Washington, The Brookings Institute.

Davies B., Anderson L. (1992) *Opting for Self Management: The early experience of Grant Maintained Schools,* London, Routledge.

Department for Education, (1994) *Consultative Circular on the Supply of School Places,* London, Department for Education.

Ernest P. (1991) *The Philosophy of Mathematics,* Basingstoke, The Falmer Press.

Fowler S. (1993) *Communities, Organisations and People,* Pro Rege, Dordt College.

Gilligan C. (1982) *In a Different Voice: Psychological Theory and Women's Development,* Cambridge MA, Harvard University Press.

Giroux H. (1983) *Theory and Resistance in Education,* London, Heinemann.

Green H. (1992) *Leadership, Values and Site Based Management,* Paper presented to the BEMAS Conference, Bristol.

Greeley A.& Rossi P. (1966) *The Education of Catholic Americans,* Chicago, Aldine Press.

Greer J.(1985) Viewing the 'other side' in Northern Ireland: Openness and Attitudes to Religion among Catholic and Protestant Adolescents, *Journal for the Scientific Study of Religion,* 24,3, pp 275-292.

Greer J.& McElhinney E.(1984) The Project on Religion in Ireland' an experiment in reconstruction, *Lumen Vitae,* 39, 3, pp 331-342.

Greer J.& McElhinney E.(1985) *Irish Christianity: A Guide for Teachers,* Dublin, Gill & Macmillan.

Hargreaves A. (1994) *Changing Teachers Changing Times,* London, Cassell.

Hodgkinson C. (1991) *Educational Leadership: The Moral Art,* Albany, University of New York Press.

Holmes M. (1992) *Educational Policy for the Pluralist Democracy: The Common School, Choice and Diversity,* London, The Falmer Press.

Hoyle E. (1986) *The Politics of School Management,* London, Hodder and Stoughton.

Hornsby-Smith M.(1978) *Catholic Education: The Unobtrusive Partner,* London, Sheed & Ward.

Lambert I. (1993) *The New Christian Schools Movement in Britain - A Case Study,* Phd Thesis, Cambridge University.

Lawton D. (1989) *Education, Culture and the National Curriculum,* London, Hodder and Stoughton.

MacDonald M., (1977) *Culture, Class and the Curriculum,* (E202 Schooling and Society: Unit 16) Milton Keynes, Open University Press.

MacIntyre A. (1992) The Virtues, the Unity of Human Life and the Concept of a Tradition, in Sandel M.(ed) *Liberalism and its Critics,* Oxford, Blackwell.

McKenzie P. (1994) *The New Christian Schools Movement,* PhD Thesis, University of Reading.

Mill J. (1859) *On Liberty,* London, Longmans.

Nias J.,Southworth G.,Yeomans R. (1989) *Staff Relationships in the Primary School,* London, Cassell.

Noddings N. (1984) *Caring: A Feminine Approach to Ethics and Moral Education,* Berkeley CA, University of California Press.

Norman R. (1993) *I Did It My Way: Some Thoughts on Autonomy,* Papers on the Philosophy of Education Society of Great Britain, April 16.

Parajes M., (1992) Teachers Beliefs and Educational Research: Cleaning Up a Messy Construct, *Review of Educational Research,*3,301-332.

Poyntz C.,& Walford G., (1994) The New Christian Schools: a Survey, *Educational Studies,*20,1,127-143.

Rawls J. (1971) *A Theory of Justice,* Cambridge Mass., Harvard University Press.

Rokeach M. (1968) *Beliefs, Attitudes and Values,* London, Jossey-Bass Inc.

Sampson E. (1989) The Challenge of Social Change for Psychology: Globalisation and Psychology's Theory of the Person, *American Psychologist,* 44,914-921.

Sandel M. (1984) The Procedural Public and the Unencumbered Self, *Political Theory* 12,pp81-96.

Sergiovanni T. (1983) *Moral Leadership: Getting to the Heart of School Improvement,* San Francisco, Jossey Bass.

Shweder R. (1982) *Beyond Self-Constructed Knowledge: the Study of Culture and Morality,* Merril-Palmer Quarterly, 28,41-69.

Swann M. (1985) *Education for All,* London, HMSO.

Tappan M. (1991) Narrative, Language and Moral Experience, *Journal of Moral Education,* 20,3.

Theissen E.(1987) Educational Pluralism and Tolerance, *Journal of Educational Thought,* 21,2.

Walford G. (1994) The New Religious Grant Maintained Schools, *Educational Management and Administration,* 22,2,123-130.

Walford G.,(ed) (1991) The Reluctant Private Sector: of Small Schools, People and Politics, in *Private Schooling, Tradition, Change and Diversity,* London, Paul Chapman Ltd.

Wertsch J. (1989) A sociocultural Approach to Mind, in Daman W.(ed) *Child Development Today and Tomorrow,* San Francisco, Jossey Bass.

West S. (1993) *Educational Values for School Leadership,* London, Kogan Page.

Williams R. (1992)(2nd edn) *The Long Revolution,* London, The Hogarth Press.

Witheral C.& Pope Edwards C.(1991) Moral versus Social-Conventional Reasoning: a Narrative and Cultural Critique, *Journal of Moral Education,* 20,3,293-303.

Young M.,& Whitty G.,(eds) (1977) *Society State and Schooling,* Lewes, Falmer Press.

Steiner Schools in Ireland:
A Case Study of Opting in

Paddy McEvoy

Support will come: on the arm of time

'Truth always lags last, limping along on the arm of time', wrote Balthasar Gracian wisely in 1647. Rudolf Steiner, in his lectures and writings, presented a radically new departure in educational thinking and practice, the breadth and depth of which are a challenge to our time. When I came to Steiner/Waldorf Education in England, having spent over twenty years teaching in state schools, the thought struck me "Why is this the best kept educational secret of the 20th century?" The answer lies in an interplay of internal and external factors. What is undeniable is the fact that the service we hope to render to the community cannot come without public/state support. Public funding will be a vindication and an affirmation of what we are doing, and hope to do. The debate on state recognition and support has gone on in the Holywood Rudolf Steiner School since its founding in the mid 1970's, and in the other Steiner/Waldorf schools in Ireland, in Co. Clare and in Dublin, since their founding in the 1980's. The Holywood School came into existence at a critical point in Northern Ireland's history. The 'Troubles' were at a relatively early, but ugly, stage and the Waldorf school provided an environment so new, so radical, that many parents welcomed it with open arms. Here was a school defined by what it was, and not by what it was not - few Catholics were in state schools, very few Protestants were in Catholic schools. There was no hidden curriculum, subtly or otherwise, socializing children into one tribal allegiance or another. A school that embodied, out of conviction, notions such as cultural diversity, parity of esteem, freedom from labelling (phrases that have become buzz-words in the sometimes phoney latter-day exchanges in the context of Education for Mutual Understanding, a cross-curricular theme accompanying the new Common Curriculum), should have been hailed as a mould-breaker by a far-sighted government. Alas, this was not to be, for Northern Ireland's first integrated school.

One is not met on entering the school with portrait of either Queen or Pope. One could not detect on reading the school's literature, biases in favour of crown or harp. The poetry of all linguistic streams can be found on the school's bookshelves; the history of both traditions is presented without favour. Parents of a child interviewed for the nursery stated that the fact that the school was in existence influenced them in having a family. When one begins to hear statements such as that, one realises the significance of one's presence in a divided society. Our older students can talk freely about their family history and be accepted while still enunciating ideas that register deeply with classmates. Our first generation of parents were quick to realise that here was a school that offered a new kind of harbour, a new kind of anchorage. Except in the Integrated Schools where Catholic and Protestant children are educated together and which are steadily growing in number, initiatives such as Education for Mutual Understanding can only progress at a snail's pace when most schools are largely culturally monolithic. The buzz words are 'parity of esteem', 'cultural diversity' and so on. The curriculum has been 're-fashioned' to ensure an end to notions of bias and discrimination and a phasing out of the downgrading of minority culture. Accusations of cultural, political engineering have been levelled at enthusiasts for integration by opponents for presuming to use schools as centres in which to attempt to solve society's ills. As someone who has taught for many years in multi-cultural schools, it is certainly a more credible exercise to present cultures in a living way when representatives of those cultures are in one's very classroom, but the fact remains that the child's deeper needs are not necessarily met because everyone wears shamrock on St. Patrick's Day, or lights candles at Diwali. The Steiner curriculum is quintessentially a multi-cultural curriculum, that validates the child and the child's cultural background without downgrading other cultures.

The Holywood Steiner School might have been hailed as a mould breaker when it arrived in 1974 had the government been on the lookout for a radically new initiative. One sees regular reference to Lagan College in Belfast as Northern Ireland's first integrated school. The Holywood Steiner School was, in fact, the province's first integrated school, albeit not government funded. The Holywood Steiner School's experience is similar to many other radical initiatives in society in the sense that recognition will only come when the case becomes irresistible. It is our responsibility to make an irresistible case for support for our education. There are many who are sympathetic to our cause. We are, however, in a position where most of our energies are deployed in school work and little is left for 'political' work. It is my view, nevertheless, that we are pushing at an open door on the matter of state funding. We must take every opportunity to present to authorities and local communities what our schools are like, and with support, could be like. Parents have a vital role to play in this process. By their fruits you shall know them.

But how are those authorities impressed when what the law dictates puts us 'beyond the pale'? We have had numerous meetings with the Department of Education in Northern Ireland over the years. One thing we find is that the change in Departmental personnel necessitates the formation of new relationships, almost on a yearly basis. And it is in the slipstream of good relationships that support will come.

The school wasn't long in existence when approaches to the Department of Education were made raising the question of public funding. A debate took place in the school, both sides of the question being represented. The more traditional school of thought presented the view that state funding is inimical to Rudolf Steiner's vision for the schools. According to this analysis, education should be independent of the state and not treated as a political football by politicians; teachers should be seen as artists/artisans rather than civil servants carrying out the whims of politicians, 'delivering' a disputed curriculum. It was also stated that once our independence was gone a vital spark would die. The proponents of public funding would point out the compromises we already live with, in view of the serious underfunding of most of our schools and our inability to serve society in any meaningful way in consequence of our insignificance. It is to be hoped that through public funding, the vital spark will become a living flame influencing the lives of thousands of children as is the case in other countries.

The school was inspected in 1991, and formal registration granted in October 1993. We applied formally in 1994 for grant maintained status (not to be confused with grant maintained status in England and Wales - The G. M. S. status in Northern Ireland is the heading under which the Catholic schools are maintained - there is no question of opting-out. We wish to opt-in!)

Why opt in? This is a vexed question. Why, when we enjoy an almost unfettered existence within a 'liberal' state, seek to jeopardise that freedom by proactively attempting to come under the state's umbrella, particularly at a time when that state prescribes the curriculum to be taught in all funded schools? This is a fundamental question that exercises the minds of those connected with Waldorf education on a daily basis. Images of tidal waves and juggernauts are often invoked by the opponents to the quest for state support, and imaginations are often overwrought earlier, rather than later, in discussion.

It is being increasingly recognised that the strengths that have accrued to us by virtue of being espoused by a certain interest group in British education in the 20th century has had its down side. The public school mentality has, while emphasising the merits of independence, also perpetuated an, if not elitist, certainly exclusivist mentality.

How different things might have been if, after the war, the decision had been taken to locate a Steiner/Waldorf flagship school in London, rather than in Forest Row, Sussex, and to press for government funding. When Waldorf schools in the rest of Europe were forging ahead in forming relationships with their respective states, we in Britain were developing a mentality of suspicion in relation to the state, no doubt influenced by people who had had bad experiences in Europe, particularly Germany, in the 1930's. This early suspicion can be gleaned from articles in our journals which, instead of grasping the nettle of local authority/state contact, questioned the wisdom of exposing the tender shoot of Waldorf Education to the depredations of the intrusive state (capitalism was bad, but socialism was worse).

In our magazines of the post war period and latterly, one encounters quote after quote from Rudolf Steiner emphasising freedom from the state and professional autonomy for schools and teachers. What one does not read often enough are quotations chosen to underline our responsibilities to the educational life of society generally, a willingness to keep in touch with developments in State education, and our excitement at sharing what we have to offer. The mentality was abroad that things are progressively getting worse in State schools, and when they get really dreadful, the state will turn to us and we will arrive on our white chargers and redeem the situation. While there may be a grain of truth in this point of view, it nevertheless behoves us to be proactive in courageously clutching the nettle of involvement with the world rather than leading a hermetically-sealed existence. By leading a detached life our ability to communicate with the world atrophies. We must learn to talk to the world in the language of the world, and if that involves talking about attainment targets, and key stages then so be it (but attainment targets and key stages that are concerned with the child's welfare, not the position of the school in a league table!).

An old ballad of the 1790's during the time of the United Irishmen states, 'Church and State in close embrace, is a burden on the human race'. Steiner education, with its emphasis on freedom from church and state, presents for the first time in the educational history of Ireland a truly free choice. With the deepening of peace, that desire for freedom from the twin 'tyrannies' of church and state is a further reason why the Steiner option must be made available to people in this country, North and South.

As part of our on-going negotiations, the Department of Education for Northern Ireland (DENI) in 1994 presented us with the main legislative areas with which we must comply before GMS is granted. These areas are:

- School Management Structures;
- The Curriculum;
- Numerical viability;
- Qualification of Teachers;
- Charges (fees) in Grant Aided Schools;
- Open enrolment;
- Publication of information;
- Assessment;
- Days of Operation.

The more problematic areas for a Steiner school are: The Curriculum; Assessment; and perhaps Management Structures. Management Structures do not seem to be an area of great difficulty. Indeed the Curriculum has emerged, in the response from DENI as the area of most difficulty. The Department has informed us that 'as statutory regulations, there is no discretion for the Department either to amend them (ie. the above conditions), or to set them aside'. The Holywood school had expressed the hope that there would be room for negotiation on the Curriculum. We have been informed that there is no room for such negotiation, while demonstrating that our students perform on a par, at least, with peers in GCSE exams, if not exceeding regional norms. The Department also states that the Holywood school 'cannot be considered for acceptance as a grant-aided school unless it can provide clear evidence that it is effectively delivering the minimum requirements of the curriculum as enshrined in legislation'.

The question is, 'What are the minimum requirements' of the Northern Ireland curriculum'? A good lawyer could have fun with that statement. Can it be that funding will be withheld because we are not 'delivering' the minimum requirements of the National Curriculum? The question of the Curriculum is a vexed one for all of our schools, largely because what we see presented as a National Curriculum is, in fact, closer to being a National Syllabus, arbitrarily drawn up, and arbitrarily assessed. What the country's children need is not a Common Curriculum, but a proper Curriculum.

Steiner schools are not easily pigeonholed. We are all-age, all-ability, all-class, all-race, integrated and comprehensive in every possible meaning of those words. How then are the authorities to respond to these schools for which there is no category?

It is ironic in Northern Ireland, where children are more divided and classified than anywhere else in these islands, that there is no heading under which Steiner schools can be accommodated. Here children are segregated by age, sex, ability and religion (social class?). The Holywood Steiner school arrives for funding, observing none of the neat segregations stipulated by law and not following the National Curriculum. What a headache we must pose for the authorities? Nevertheless we have received tolerance and forbearance from officialdom. Not much warmth or encouragement, but then no official wishes to be quoted as having said, 'You stand a good chance of funding.' At a recent meeting with representatives of the Department of Education, we asked the question, 'Are we wasting our time with this application?' There was a pause, but we were told unequivocally to press ahead with the application; that there wasn't a great chance we would achieve it under present circumstances, but it would be untrue to say there was no chance.

Inspectors are a curious breed. They are generally people who left the classroom because they were fired by a zeal to enhance the quality of the education service by seeing to it that 'good practice' be extended to every nook and cranny of every classroom in the land. When 'good practice' became the catch-phrase of the new orthodoxy in the seventies and eighties, it was regarded with suspicion by long-serving professional teachers who understood by it that good practice would come to mean doing it the state's way. Nowadays, we hear the good practice catch-cry cropping up in business, prisons, hospitals, and factories, etc., and it means 'doing it our way', reducing all activity to that which is measurable. Confidence in the individual's ability and motivation to do his or her best out of his or her own moral choice is harder and harder to find. The concept of people working out of their own volition, autonomously motivated to act in the best interests of children, on very meagre resources, is a notion that the inspectors who came to our school found difficult to understand. We generally do not find what we are looking for unless we believe it is there, and the inspectors, guided by notions of 'good practice' elsewhere had, in our opinion, difficulty in appreciating many of what we would consider the strengths in our way of doing things. Again, it is a matter of the whole being greater than the sum of the parts. Neither did we want officials to come in and say all is perfect. We are only too painfully aware of the consequences of underfunding in areas of staffing, in-service training, facilities, and premises, but we wish to improve our performance within the context of becoming better Waldorf/Steiner schools rather than jettisoning what we are, and adopting the state's 'good practice'.

With regard to the situation in the Republic of Ireland, the Irish Steiner Schools Association is in contact with the Department of Education in Dublin to pursue the matter of funding for our two schools in the South, in Dublin and in Co. Clare. To date the Minister, Mrs. Niamh Breathnach, has informed us that we do not meet the criteria laid down for qualifying for public funding in Eire. Having enquired as to what precisely these criteria are, the Department is in the process of responding to our request for clarification.

Another aspect of our dealings with the Irish Government is that a parent of the Cooleenbridge, Co. Clare School has decided to challenge the government on constitutional grounds, on its refusal to fund the Clare School. At present a case is being prepared by a local solicitor, Mr. Billy Loughnane. According to the constitution of the Republic of Ireland, parents have clearly delineated rights with regard to the education of their children. There is an absence of a legislative tradition in Southern education, hence the difficulty in being specific on the criteria that must be met, one of which is that a school must be denominationally classifiable - hence a state-funded Muslim school in Dublin. There is a growing number of interest groups directly involved in educational practice and provision in the Republic of Ireland, and the Steiner schools are clearly one of these interest groups. It remains to be seen whether the Government will risk losing a high profile constitutional case.

The Steiner schools in Ireland are seeking to take their place as another option for parents and their children in this rapidly changing island. Society is in a state of flux, North and South - the final resolution of deep issues is being tackled for the first time in the modern history of the island. Ireland is experiencing a Reformation, a Renaissance of native cultural impulses, and a re-embracing of external cultural forms; an industrial and agricultural revolution; a demand by women for a new role; an extraordinary demographic situation where an estimated 50% of the population is under 25 years of age. Into this maelstrom of uncertainty, where political and religious verities are questioned as never before, arrives Steiner education, willing to play its part. If we are to play a significant role in this country, North and South, we must do it from a position of public recognition, support and accountability. With funding will come a new constellation of challenges, but the new energies and scale of operations will enable us to train, recruit, and hold teachers of the highest calibre, whose career prospects are secure, who can rely on proper pension provisions, who can embrace continuing professional and personal development, who will run schools that will be a beacon in a disorderly world.

What benefits would flow to the local community as a consequence of the funding of Steiner Schools? The Holywood School differs from the normal integrated school in a number of ways. When we considered applying for maintained status in the 1980's, it was felt that Grant Maintained Integrated Status was the correct heading under which we should apply for funding. When we asked for advice on this question we were told that, to apply for funding under the Integrated heading, we would encounter a further 'raft of legislation'. Part of that legislation would be the need to satisfy quotas of Catholic/Protestants in qualifying for funding. We would have been required to discover the religious background of our parents to demonstrate that we were 'integrated'. As the concept of integration in a Steiner School is a much more involved notion than headcounting, we decided to seek funding as a maintained school with the option of becoming an Integrated school at a later date, when hopefully quotas are less stridently sought, and a deeper appreciation of our ethos was a reality. There are quite a number of people in Northern Ireland whose ties with traditional faiths/allegiances are loosening, if not loosened. These are people who do not identify with the Catholic/Protestant integration model of social change. They are privately saying 'a plague on both your houses'. These people have their children currently in Catholic/State/Integrated schools and are required to pay lip-service to, either overt, or not well-hidden agenda that label their children. The Steiner school would provide an option where the believer, or non-believer, could send his/her child, knowing that the inner needs of the child were being catered for in a non-denominational way, and that the freedom of the child to make eventual decisions about religious and spiritual matters was respected.

To allow a Steiner school under the state umbrella would be the ultimate breaking of the State mould. In our dealings with educational authorities we are, and must be, utterly open in informing them of the step they are taking, because it will be the most radical educational step taken by government in this century, or for the foreseeable future.

In being able to opt for a maintained Steiner school, parents can begin to align a series of complex options that can only be aligned through the Steiner option. These involve psychological, moral, spiritual, economic and social criteria. Our 'high-flying' students share classrooms with those with learning difficulties, blacks with whites, the well-off with the economically deprived, Protestant with Catholic, girl with boy.

A desirable consequence of funding would be that it would be good for our children to be no longer seen as 'different', and to be able to more easily participate in inter-schools' activities. With funding, our schools could be two-form entry, which would make a fully developed school cater for 600 - 700 pupils, a user-friendly size which is being recognised as an ideal number for the maintenance of living relationships. From listening to parents' concerns about the dubious pressures placed on their children, it is more than likely that our schools will be over-subscribed when funding is made available.

Truth indeed lags last and in these wayward times it is urgently incumbent upon us to enunciate our truth. The question is not so much 'Will we secure government funding?', as 'When will we secure government funding?' When there is sufficient consciousness and will to serve the deeper needs of the wider community, and to publicly declare what our needs are in making that service a reality, I believe recognition and funding will follow.

Muslim Schools in England and Wales

Ibrahim Hewitt

In the name of Allah, The Most Merciful, The Most Kind

When you hear or read the words 'Muslim school', what images are conjured up? Would you expect to see a 'school for trainee Ayatollahs', as one well-known member of parliament did before visiting a Muslim school in London a few years back? If so, I am afraid you are likely to be disappointed for, as that same MP said after his visit, the average Muslim school 'is just like other schools.'

Up to a point, this is good PR for us, but it also begs the question, what is different and why the call for such schools? And why should they be funded from the public purse?

The fact is, a well-run Muslim school must be visited to *feel* the difference that an Islamic ethos can make. One school in Bradford has received letters from local further education institutions praising the school on the calibre of its students, not just in academic terms but also in human terms. In short, they are very pleasant students, well-mannered, hard-working and responsive to their surroundings. It is - supporters of Muslim schools would argue - the fact that they can grow and study in an educational environment conducive and sympathetic to their faith, which allows them to be confident as Muslims in a pluralistic society, and thus be at ease with themselves and with others. For young Muslims, many of whom face almost intolerable pressures to conform to two conflicting sets of values at crucial stages of their lives, within and without the home, such an environment can be their lifeline. By successfully bridging the ever-widening gap between traditional values in the home and peer-group pressures found in a secularist state school system, Muslim schools have hit on a formula which is more attractive to parents and students alike. They are also proving their worth in terms of quality, standards and levels of achievement. As for being cost-effective... well, you only have to look at their external examination results and per capita expenditure; most achieve better results with less than an eighth of the budgets allocated to state funded schools through LMS (local management of schools).

Muslim schools have grown in number since the early eighties, over a period when state education has become ever more politicised, and they are to be found all over the country. They exist in expected places such as Bradford, Birmingham and London, and in not so expected places like Gloucester, Retford and Crowborough. Today there are around 40 full-time schools spread across England (most) and Wales (one). They are being run in premises ranging from purpose-built buildings to portacabins, and varying in size, pupil numbers and primary or secondary phases.

What are the attractions? For some parents the main reason for opting to send their children - in particular, their daughters - to a Muslim school is as a form of refuge from a state system they believe (not without reason) is breaking down and failing them. Muslims in some parts of Britain (notably Tower Hamlets in the East End of London) are consistently at the bottom of the pile when it comes to academic achievement. In part, it could be argued, this is due to the fact that education plays little or no part in the lives of the parents, many of whom come from rural backgrounds in South Asia, and this disinterest is passed on; young Muslims from such homes are given little or no encouragement to study beyond what is legally necessary. This does not disguise the fact, however, that many Muslims face a degree of harassment from every level of the education hierarchy leading, for example, to the School Curriculum and Assessment Authority (SCAA) setting the date for school tests on the day of the major Muslim festival of Eidul Adha in May 1995. This was despite SCAA being informed of the likely day of the festival ('give or take a day or so') at least two years in advance.

Incidents like this do not increase Muslim parents' confidence in British state education system they, like almost everyone else, were brought up to believe was 'the best in the world'.

Such prejudice is encountered by *practising* Muslim teachers in the state system, so much so that it is rare to find them in senior positions in schools or local education authorities (LEAs), or the

Department for Education (DFE) itself. Muslim schools, on the other hand, offer sincere Muslim teachers the opportunity for advancement, personally and professionally. They, in turn, serve as prime role models for their students, demonstrating that a person does not have to jettison any semblance of religious practice to study at higher levels, gain valuable qualifications and move into a successful career. The fear that their children will divest themselves of their faith, almost unconsciously, because of the afore-mentioned peer-group pressures and unreasonable pressure from secularised teachers ('Why do you want to fast? It won't do you any good!') is very real for a growing number of Muslim parents. Admittedly, not every Muslim takes their faith so much to heart; the same is true of supposed adherents of all faiths. But whereas those Christians and Jews who desire faith-based educational provision for their children have schools paid for by the state, Muslims (and other faith groups) have no such option. Not one of our institutions as yet receives funding from the government. Britain is lagging behind some of its European partners in this respect; Holland, Denmark and Ireland, to name but three, all fund Muslim schools within their respective education systems.[1]

As with any educational provision, finance plays a huge part in the life of Muslim schools; it is a crucial factor for governors, teachers, pupils (who face shortages of adequate resources in cash-strapped schools), parents (who must dig deep to find school fees) and prospective parents (who sweat over how they are going to pay school fees). Indeed, although the number of Muslim children attending Muslim schools is relatively small (around 5,000), and this is used as an argument for the 'fact' that the overwhelming majority of the community do not want them, it is true to say that if Muslim schools were paid for by the state, through the taxes Muslims as British citizens pay, far more parents would opt to enrol their children.[2] Given a realistic choice, I am confident that most Muslims would choose state funded, faith specific community schools. This is borne out by the fact that in the absence of a viable Muslim school in their area many choose to send their children to Anglican or Roman Catholic schools. The religious ethos, even of a different religion, is important. The lack of credible finance cannot be ruled out, therefore, as a major limiting factor on the numbers of pupils on roll in Muslim schools.

Since 1944, 'any persons' in England and Wales have had the right to establish schools and apply for them to be paid for by the state (1944 Education Act, section 13). Subsequent legislation (notably the 1993 Education Act) has reinforced that principle, and extended the choice on offer from voluntary aided to grant maintained schools. At the time of writing (mid-1995) two Muslim schools have applied for voluntary aided status; both were turned down by a government which is supposed to hold 'parental choice' as a major plank of its education policy. The reasons given were, in the minds of most observers, spurious. Why, for example, did surplus places in local state schools prevent state funding for Islamia Primary School in Brent but not the establishment of City Technology colleges around the country, or the approval of grant maintained status for schools earmarked for closure by LEAs? And why have two Catholic secondary schools been granted GM status subject to there being 'minor alterations' in their admissions criteria but Feversham College in Bradford cannot be given VA status subject to minor alterations in Health and Safety procedures? Such leeway appears to be selective; if they are so important, why were such deficiencies in those procedures not picked up in successive inspections by Her Majesty's Inspectors?

Muslims feel aggrieved when such bias is shown towards genuine community efforts to make positive contributions towards the education of their children within the framework of English Law. No Muslim school has ever asked for special treatment, merely equal treatment, but even this, it seems, is too much for the British Government

Contradictions abound in the arguments against state funding of Muslim schools (against Muslim schools *per se*, in fact), fuelling the growing belief that the Muslim community is facing discrimination from the highest levels of government down. Since religious discrimination is not a crime in mainland Britain (it is in Northern Ireland), this is one of the hardest things to prove and overcome.

Misconceptions abound, aided and abetted by a media preferring a subjective stance instead of objectivity in coverage. Muslim schools, we are frequently told, are 'Asian' schools and are, thus, ill-equipped to prepare children for life in a multi-cultural society. Even left-of-centre critics stoop to such a stereotypical view, displaying their ignorance of the nature of the

Muslim community which is actually multi-cultural in its own right. Muslims from every corner of the globe enrich the community with regional and national traditions built on the shared values, beliefs and practices of Islam. Local demography being what it is, there are, of course, some Muslim schools which are 'Asian' in character; Islamia Primary School a few years ago, though, had 23 different nationalities represented among 100 pupils and staff. That is not unique.

The 'voluntary apartheid' objections follow-on from this argument but race never has - and never will be - one of the entrance criteria for Muslim schools, unlike (and this is a highly controversial issue) Jewish schools, 20+ of which are state funded. Fear of the 'anti-Semitic' label pushes the reality of state funded, 'separate' Jewish education out of the question; people tend to gloss over the issue as if these schools are an irrelevance to the overall discussion. But they are not, for a number of reasons.

First, Jewish schools set a precedent for non-Christian schools funded by the taxpayer; second, they are very popular with parents and pupils alike; third, they are usually very successful academically. All three points are applicable to the debate on state funding for Muslim schools and yet are summarily dismissed with statements like, 'This is a Christian country [sic] with Judaeo-Christian traditions', and 'Muslims must integrate and they cannot do that with separate schools.' Show me a minority (and remember, there are estimated to be five Muslims in Britain for every Jew) which has integrated into every level of British society more successfully than the Jewish community. And this is despite (or because of?) the proliferation of Jewish schools, Jewish welfare organisations, in fact, a whole social structure tailored for the community's needs! If state funds can be provided for this, why should Muslims be denied an equal opportunity for such success?

However, Muslims do not want state money simply because others do. Indeed, it is not just money schools are after (although it would be welcome in most cases!). Some of the schools are content to stay independent and if the local community can afford to support the school, fine. What they would like to see is a more equitable approach to Muslim schools in matters such as planning and building control. Finding suitable premises is difficult, and even when school buildings become surplus to LEA requirements there is - with one or two notable exceptions - much reluctance to help struggling Muslim schools by selling or leasing them to the local community. Could there be political motives behind such decisions?[3] Maybe; after all, a Muslim school moving into a purpose-built building doesn't need planning permission, and refusing such permission has been one method employed by local authorities to check our progress, restricting the scope for development.

Time for a cliché: Islam is a complete way of life. This includes education and we believe that Islam can make a valuable contribution to all subjects on the timetable. It could be argued that a broad, balanced Islamic curriculum meets the requirements of the 1988 Education Reform Act to provide for the 'spiritual, moral, cultural, mental and physical development of pupils... and of society' (Section 1[2]) even more than the largely secular National Curriculum, because spirituality, morals and culture are not limited to the RE class.

Being pragmatic, if nothing else, most Muslim schools follow the state curriculum as far as possible, introducing Islamic elements when appropriate. All are visited regularly by official inspectors and must maintain good standards. This requires adequate resources, however, and so we come full circle back to the need for money. The Muslim community is not exceptionally wealthy and many parents on dwindling incomes struggle to pay school fees for what they believe should be provided by the state.

There is a good case to put for bringing 'traditional' values and alternative methodology into a mainstream education service which is desperately in need of fresh ideas. As more and more parents across a broad spectrum of faith and value systems come to understand this and seek to start their own schools, Muslims are realising that they are not, after all, alone in their quest for an education for their children which, in spirit as well as practice, ensures that 'pupils are to be educated in accordance with the wishes of their parents' (1944 Education Act, section 76). To that could be added, 'unless they are Muslims.' Quite whether the Secretary of State for Education sees it that way is still unresolved.

1   Holland has 30 Muslim schools, three Hindu schools, two Jewish schools and 4,862 Christian schools of various denominations (Source: The Netherlands Ministry of Education and Science, 1994). Denmark has 10 Muslim schools among a wide range of private

schools which receive state grants, including Christian schools, 'progressive free schools' and Rudolf Steiner schools (Source: *Private Schools in Denmark,* Ministry of Education and Research, 1992). The Republic of Ireland has one state funded Muslim school in the capital, Dublin.

2   The results of a survey carried out in Manchester in 1989 showed that 'only a quarter of the [Muslim] girls [surveyed] favoured' Muslim schools (Times Educational Supplement, 24.3.89). The others, it was claimed, were 'overwhelmingly against the idea', therefore Muslim schools were/are not a good idea. However, transferred into national population terms that adds up to around 60,000 Muslim girls supporting Muslim schools (as well as, incidentally, half of the parents interviewed). Britain is clearly lagging some way behind in the state funded Muslim schools' stakes!

3   A document dated 1 September 1987 drawn up by Kirklees Local Education Authority officers for elected members considering the application for voluntary aided status made by Zakaria Muslim Girls' School in Batley contained an interesting sentence: 'More difficult to gauge are the less direct effects and the *ideological* (my emphasis) consequences which would follow the establishment of the Authority's first aided school which has Islam as its ethos.' By the following July, when the document was made public, 'ideological' had been expunged. I can't imagine why.

Denationalising the Curriculum: From Bureaucratic Monolith to Safety-Net

James Tooley

Introduction

The government cannot win over the National Curriculum. Two years ago, recognising the monstrosity it had created, it appointed Sir Ron Dearing to slim down the curriculum and simplify testing. But his proposals only led to an intensification of educationalists' frustration and anger. The English subject advisory committee is protesting strongly about the way its advice was ignored; the primary working group finds itself 'profoundly dispirited' about the new curriculum for the under sevens (*Times Educational Supplement* May 20th 1994); the revised History curriculum is criticised, for not making significant events in British History compulsory (The Times 28th February 1994), or for selling out to the 'Right' (*Times Educational Supplement* 4th March 1994); the original mathematics working group is publicly asking for the mathematical *status quo* to be maintained and the Dearing slim-down to be resisted; both the Centre for Policy Studies and the National Union of Teachers - peculiar bedfellows - have condemned Dearing's proposals for still being over-bureaucratic and time-consuming. Whichever way the government turns, it will encounter resistance: the deep-rooted problem is that the technical requirements and nature of education are not compatible with government control of the curriculum[1].

However, all is not lost for those who dislike this current National Curriculum, or are uncomfortable with the notion of a national curriculum in general. In this chapter I explore two ways in which schools could opt-out of the National Curriculum. The proposals *require no significant new legislation:* the requirements are already in place within the 1988 Education Reform Act. They are cost-effective, practical, and elegantly simple proposals which would restore professional integrity to teachers and autonomy to schools, divert funds back to the 'chalk face' and away from the Schools Curriculum and Assessment Authority (SCAA), while at the same time promoting innovation, high standards, parental choice, and accountability. By permitting schools to opt-out of the National Curriculum, the government would encourage choice and diversity - its avowed educational goals - while restoring the National Curriculum to its intended 'safety-net' purpose, to ensure that no school fails to provide an entitlement curriculum.

The solution to the problem of the nationalised curriculum lies in the little-noticed Sections 16 and 17 of the 1988 Education Reform Act. (The specifications of these are included in the Appendix). Section 16 permits schools to apply to the Secretary of State to opt out of the National Curriculum, in part or in whole. Section 17 allows the Secretary of State to authorise *any* departure from the National Curriculum, by regulation.

Who might be interested in using these methods of opting out? Several types of schools suggest themselves. Firstly, the mechanisms might be of particular interest to any private schools seeking to 'opt in' to Grant Maintained (GM) status under the 1993 Education Act. I know of a Steiner school, for instance, which would be very keen on becoming a GM school, but which could only do so at present if it was prepared to give up its long-established innovative curriculum; under my suggestions, such a school could apply to opt-out of the National Curriculum at the same time as it seeks to opt-in to GM status. Secondly, there could be schools which felt that some adaptation of the curriculum would satisfy parental demand, or those that saw a curriculum 'niche' that could bring about increased demand for, or improved quality of the education they offered their children. Such a school might wish to offer greater flexibility, perhaps, to its less able students in terms of vocational courses, or to academically extend its more able students. Or a school might want to seek to do innovative work with new technology. Thirdly, it must be clear that if schools could opt-out of the National Curriculum, then this would be a way of opting out of national testing (SATs), as the National Curriculum is the syllabus for the SATs; perhaps some schools who could argue that national testing was undermining the educational process might also seek to opt-out - although they would be unlikely to be able to use one of the methods outlined below, for reasons which will become apparent.

My proposals follow two paths: the *'standard track'* component uses Section 16, while the *'fast-track'* uses Section 17.

Denationalising the curriculum

The 'standard track'

The first opt-out route uses Section 16. For this route, the existing legislation itself is all that is required - no new regulations or orders are needed. For Section 16 presents, *as it stands,* a clear, unambiguous loophole in the application of the National Curriculum. The clause reads that, for the purpose of 'development work' or 'experiments', schools are permitted to apply to the Secretary of State for Education to opt-out of the curriculum, and these are sufficiently broad terms to cover a variety of eventualities. Almost *any* change to a school's curriculum can be described as 'development work', as was acknowledged by the government in the Act's passage through Parliament. So no new legislation is required and schools could, right now, start to use this process to opt-out. What would aid the process, however, would be for the government to publicise the existence of Section 16, and for schools to be reassured that applications will be sympathetically handled. Now the wording of Section 16(3) (see appendix) means that there would be different routes for Grant Maintained (GM) schools and other maintained schools. GM schools using this route would simply have to apply to the Secretary of State; other maintained schools would first have to apply to their Local Education Authority (LEA), who would forward applications to the Secretary of State.

Importantly, under Section 16, permitting schools to opt-out of the National Curriculum is *at the discretion* of the Secretary of State; this would remain the case in my opt-out proposals, although it would be expected that he or she would sympathetically consider each case on its merits, and that there would be no unreasonable refusals.

Upon opting out of the National Curriculum, a proportion of the budget of the Schools Curriculum and Assessment Authority

(SCAA) - the curriculum quango - would be allocated to the school, for purposes of curriculum development and assessment.

The 'fast-track'

The Secretary of State for Education, by regulation, creates a category of schools named perhaps the 'Approved Curriculum' (AC) schools. This category describes schools which are either (a) oversubscribed, or (b) have sufficient demand to fill all their pupil places. By specifying such schools under regulation, the Secretary of State can then use Section 17 of the 1988 Education Reform Act to allow for the National Curriculum not to apply to AC schools.

Schools fulfilling either of the specified requirements are then invited - there is no compulsion - to apply for AC status. On application by the governing body of the school, a simple checking procedure quickly evaluates the school's records, and, if its claim is confirmed, opting-out is permitted without fuss. As with Section 16 opt-outs, a proportion of the budget of SCAA would be given to the school.

The regulations would also specify some ways in which the AC status could be revoked - and similar considerations would probably be specified when Section 16 opt-outs were considered. Firstly, if the school fails to maintain its pupil rolls at the beginning of the school year, unless it could prove that demographic changes have made this impossible to avoid, it must return to follow the National Curriculum the following year. Secondly, if a qualified majority of parents at any time vote to opt back into the National Curriculum, then the AC status is revoked. Both these mechanisms - and of course, there could be other similar ones - would ensure that accountability to parental demand would be maintained.

To summarise: the proposals here use existing legislation, and would only require the Secretary of State for Education to publicise the existence of Section 16, and to sympathetically consider any schools wishing to opt-out using it; and to make the necessary regulations regarding 'Approved Curriculum' schools for Section 17 opt-outs.

The advantages that these proposals would bring to schools are clear: schools which were popular, or had visionary leaders or innovative staff would be released from the burden of following a centrally prescribed curriculum, from the associated and burdensome administrative tasks which accompany it; those schools would also receive additional funds devolved from central government. Meanwhile, those schools which were not in the position to demonstrate their popularity, or who did not wish to be innovative around their curriculum, could still follow the National Curriculum. So the National Curriculum would remain as a 'safety net', to ensure that no school would fail to provide its pupils with an entitlement curriculum.

Objections to the proposals

There are likely to be two objections to the proposals put forward here. *Firstly*, that these proposals distort either the intentions of the government in bringing Sections 16 and 17 into the Education Reform Act, or the use to which these Sections have been put since they became law. *Secondly*, it might be argued that, without the National Curriculum applied to all schools, problems of curriculum accountability and the need for a 'broad and balanced' curriculum will arise.

The Government's intentions for and usage of Sections 16 and 17

In the case of Section 16, the first objection clearly does not hold. For Section 16 was included in the original Bill explicitly to counter fears *from all parties* that the National Curriculum was over-prescriptive and would cramp innovation. Mrs Angela Rumbold (then Minister of State at the Department of Education and Science) sought to allay these fears in Parliament: 'We feel strongly that there should be an ability to respond to developments and to changes that arise from need and circumstances... *The flexibility offered by [section 16] is needed to enable that to happen.'*[2] . Mrs Rumbold stressed that one explicit reason for drafting what was to become Section 16 was to ensure that 'desirable curriculum development work should not be hampered or curtailed by the national curriculum'. She stressed that the National Curriculum was not 'set in stone': 'We think that the Secretary of State should have the ability to suspend statutory requirements in particular cases so that he may allow desirable experimentation and development work.'[3].

So it is unequivocal that Section 16 was intended specifically to counter opposition to the centralising tendencies of the National Curriculum. Now, interestingly, Section 16 has never been used - indeed, the Department for Education has kept quiet about its existence. Not surprisingly, most educationalists are completely ignorant of it. Last year I wrote an article urging schools to use Section 16 to opt out of those parts of the National Curriculum with which they were dissatisfied (for example, the technology curriculum); among others, *The Guardian* rejected my piece: the editor haughtily replied that he was 'not in the business of encouraging teachers in a misguided attempt to defy the law', illustrating that he had no understanding of the nature of Section 16.

Interestingly, however, Sir Ron Dearing *did* mention Section 16 in his *Final Report* on slimming down the National Curriculum. There he proposed: 'Pending the introduction of a new Order for technology, I recommend that schools should be able to make application under section 16 of the Education Reform Act 1988 to teach the National Curriculum Council's recommended curriculum on an experimental basis in Key Stages 1, 2 and 3. [4]. This proposal indicates something of special significance. For Dearing is affirming that he found considerable dissatisfaction with National Curriculum technology, and that *schools should be able to express their dissatisfaction by applying to opt-out of the National Curriculum regulations* for technology - at least temporarily - using Section 16. But the government's acceptance of this proposal indicates that they too accept that Section 16 can be used by individual schools to express dissatisfaction with parts of the National Curriculum. Dearing created an important precedent, a precedent which justifies the further extension of this principle under my proposed curriculum opt-outs.

The case of Section 17 is different. It began as a technical modification to other clauses of the Education Reform Bill which catered for children with special educational needs. The language of these earlier clauses was found to be either objectionable or legally unsatisfactory, so the new clause was drafted. However, crucially, these modifications meant that the final Section 17 became of much broader application than was originally intended, indeed specifically designed to apply to pupils *without* special educational needs statements. The modifications were brought forward without dissent from the opposition, who, it seems, persisted in believing that the section still addressed special needs!

So we could say that Section 17 should not really be considered as a way of opting out of the National Curriculum, for that was not its intended purpose. However, the government has used Section 17 in similar ways to which we are proposing. It has been ready to use it in its broadest possible interpretation, to allow for flexibility in the application of the National Curriculum. Firstly, Section 17 was used to disapply pupils in Wales at Key Stage 1 from the National Curriculum requirements relating to English[5]. Then came the various provisions under the *Statutory Instruments 1992 Nos. 155-157*, relating to exemptions of pupils at Key Stage 4 (KS4). The first exempts pupils from the National Curriculum in a particular subject who have already taken an examination in that subject before the second year of KS4; if the examination was in geography or history, then the National Curriculum is disapplied for both subjects (No. 155). The second allows for pupils who are studying geography not to study history, and vice versa, (No. 156), the third exempts pupils from National Curriculum science who are studying for all three GCSEs in physics, chemistry and biology (No. 157).

Now, while the provisions for Wales, and Statutory Instruments 155 and 157 could, with some stretching of the language, be said to apply to 'special needs' children, we see, unambiguously, that No. 156 could not possibly be interpreted in this way - Section 17 was simply used to overcome the inconvenience of an over-stretched curriculum. So there is a clear precedent for using Section 17 to allow for flexibility in the application of the National Curriculum. Hence my proposed usage of it is in line with the government's own applications.

It might be objected, in the context of the proposals which I have put forward, that all of the government's applications apply to 'groups of pupils', and it is a further misapplication of the intentions of the Section to seek to apply them to schools. However, Circular 5/89 states that regulations under Section 17 'may specify the cases and circumstances of *types of schools* as well as of pupil, although the Secretary of State has at present no plans to use them for the former purpose' (para. 56, emphasis added). This allows for the type of Section 17 application envisaged in my proposals.

Hence we can conclude that the proposed uses of Sections 16 and 17 are either in line with the intentions of the government when introducing them through Parliament (Section 16) or in line with their applications (Section 17) or suggested application (Section 16) since becoming law.

Curriculum accountability and the 'broad and balanced' curriculum

The second set of objections are likely to concern the problem of curriculum accountability and the need for a 'broad and balanced' curriculum. For the whole point of the National Curriculum is that it takes individual schools' discretion away from curricular issues in order to ensure that each school is accountable on curricular matters to the government. Allowed to opt-out of the National Curriculum, schools could be free to introduce, for example, the whole gamut of anti-racist education, peace studies, and so on, loathed by the Conservative Party; or schools could offer an undemanding curriculum; or, finally, schools, in particular religious schools, might impose narrow and unbalanced curricula on their pupils - perhaps it is feared this would particularly affect girls. In all of these cases, it could be argued, the Secretary of State would be powerless to stop schools developing their curricula in this way.

Now it must be observed that there is one easy way around these problems as far the 'standard track' Section 16 opt-outs are concerned. Under that route, opting-out is at the discretion of the Secretary of State, who could, for example, specify that schools would still need to demonstrate to their local education authority that they were offering a broad and balanced curriculum - in much the same way that home-schoolers have to show this under the 1944 legislation.

It is only under the 'Fast-track' Section 17 opt-outs that the problem is likely to arise. But this is where the starkness of the choice facing the government really emerges, and indeed, where an easy rebuttal is available, on grounds offered by the government itself concerning independent schools. For Section 17 opt-out schools are popular schools. In the educational market-place they have received parental acclaim. But then - *in the government's own terms* - shouldn't this of itself ensure accountability? For this was precisely the argument put forward by the government in arguing why *independent* schools didn't have to follow the National Curriculum. Angela Rumbold pointed out that there was no need to impose a national curriculum on independent schools because they were already disciplined by the market: 'Parents are free to send their children to [private schools] if they wish, and that is a fundamental freedom. *They will do so only if the education offered by independent schools is what they want for their children. That is the discipline of market forces, and it is a real discipline'* [6].

The discipline of the market is enough to allow independent schools to maintain their independence in curricula matters. But the government has been endeavouring to establish an *internal* market in state schooling: the demand-side mechanisms of open enrolment and per capita funding have been functioning for several years now. If Mrs Rumbold's argument carried weight at the time of her making it, it carries little weight now: for the government's reforms have brought about, to a certain extent, the very situation they praised in respect of the independent sector! The internal market in education is of course imperfect. Indeed, one of its imperfections is precisely that the 'supply-side' of education needs to be opened up to allow genuine choice. And one way in which this could be facilitated is if there was flexibility around the National Curriculum, with schools genuinely being allowed to offer alternative curricula. The National Curriculum has a place, perhaps, in ensuring that less popular schools are offering an entitlement curriculum. But it has no place in prescribing the curriculum for schools which maintain popularity - *the discipline of the market can achieve this*. The government's own commitment to markets undermines this objection to allowing popular schools to opt-out of the National Curriculum.

Conclusions

There has always been a stark contradiction between the National Curriculum and the desire of government to ensure parental choice in education, and diversity of schooling opportunity. This 'distortion in logic' was pointed out to the government in the original debates in Parliament. As time goes by, the contradiction is becoming more apparent. The internal market gains hold, schools experience and value the devolved autonomy and accountability to parents and pupils on the one hand, and feel the vivid contrast between this and the heavy-handed government intervention in issues of curriculum and assessment. It is notable that it was not over issues of local management of schools or per capita funding that the major teaching unions were able to galvanise their members into recent action: it was over the imposition of the National Curriculum and national testing. The irony of this is that legislation is already in place within the very Education Act which brought about this imposition, which, with some minor additional regulations, could allow schools to opt-out of the National Curriculum and of national testing.

The National Curriculum was introduced as a regulatory discipline for schools perceived as being outside of any accountability framework. At the time of its introduction, no state schools, certainly, had the discipline of markets to contend with. But since then, the internal market has been created and is thriving. The arguments for a universal state-sponsored national curriculum have been undermined by the logic of the government's own reforms. It is time the government bit the bullet and recognised the force of its own arguments, and the power of its own reforms. A safety-net curriculum may be needed for those schools which are not flourishing; but a bureaucratic monolith only stifles the creativity and energy of teachers in many schools which already have sufficient accountability through the internal market.

Appendix: Sections 16 and 17 of the 1988 Education Reform Act

Section 16

(1) For the purpose of enabling development work or experiments to be carried out, the Secretary of State may direct as respects a particular maintained school that, for such period as may be

specified in the direction, the provisions of the National
Curriculum -
  (a) shall not apply; or
  (b) shall apply with such modifications as may be so
  specified.

(2) A direction under subsection (1) above may apply either
generally or in such cases as may be specified in the direction.

(3) A direction shall not be given under subsection (1) above
except -
  (a) in the case of a county, controlled or maintained special
  school, on an application by the local education authority
  with the agreement of the governing body or by the
  Curriculum Council with the agreement of both the local
  education authority and the governing body;
  (b) in the case of a grant-maintained, aided or special
  agreement school, on an application by the governing body or
  by the Curriculum Council with the agreement of the
  governing body.

(4) The Secretary of State may make it a condition of a direction
under subsection (1) above that any person by whom or with
whose agreement the request for the direction was made
should, when so directed or at specified intervals, report to the
Secretary of State on any matters specified by him.

(5) The Secretary of State may by a direction under this subsection
vary or revoke a direction under subsection (1) above.

Section 17

The Secretary of State may by regulations provide that the
provisions of the National Curriculum, or such of those provisions
as may be specified in the regulations -
  (a) shall not apply; or
  (b) shall apply with such modifications as may be so
  specified; in such cases or circumstances as may be so
  specified.

PART III

EDUCATION FOR
ENVIRONMENTAL
SUSTAINABILITY

Education for Sustainability

Crispin Tickell

Introduction

We are in favour of education and sustainability in the same way that we are against sin. The problem is how to put them together. Without sustainability in education, there is no prospect for sustainability anyhow or anywhere.

Sustainability

The fashionable phrase for sustainability is sustainable development, largely because development has come to be synonymous with progress, better use of human potentialities, varying degrees of industrialization, and higher living standards on the Western model. Here are some attempts at definition:

- the Brundtland Commission on sustainable development (1987); 'Development that meets the needs of the present without compromising the ability of future generations to meet their own needs'.
- Principle 1 of the Rio Declaration on Environment and Development (1992): 'Human beings are at the centre of concerns for sustainable development. They are entitled to a healthy and productive life in harmony with nature.'
- The Gladwin/Freeman definition (1994): 'Biospherically compatible and socially equitable improvement in the quality of life'.

None of these definitions is satisfactory. The first begs more questions than it answers. The second does not really help. The third is a bit of a joke. As slogans I suppose they have some value. Sometimes aggregations of thought can point in the right direction. But they are more like a jellyfish of impressions than a coherent thought process.

To my mind the greatest defect in the Brundtland definition is not the much criticised use of the word 'needs' (what are needs? and whose needs?), but rather its anthropocentricity. The world was not made for humans, and the illusion that it was is at the heart of the problem.

All concepts of sustainability must surely begin with planetary health. That health is now endangered. Before the industrial revolution, humans had already changed the face of the land, but it was a matter of warts and blemishes which could heal rather than the open surgery which has caused widening scars ever since.

These include the incredible multiplication of one animal species: our own; its rising consumption of resources and production of waste; the degradation of land and water; the changes in the chemistry of the atmosphere; and the destruction of natural biological diversity on the scale which followed the likely impact of a planetary body 65 million years ago and ended the long dominance of the dinosaurs.

Together these changes amount to an acceleration of environmental change unprecedented since humans became an identifiable animal species.

With their short lifespans most humans do not see the moving picture around them. To some extent our genes, and to some extent the culture we inherit, predetermine the way we look at problems. Together they constitute each human's world view in so far as he or she has one. Current assumptions include the following:

- greater prosperity and material welfare are good in themselves, and are therefore all embracing human targets; in the same way higher standards of living mean higher quality of life;
- it follows that economic growth on the traditional definition is also good; from this follows an apparatus of thinking about free markets, free trade, and high consumption;
- accompanying it is an almost religious belief in technology as the universal fixer of problems;

- the spread of a culture of rising expectations, nourished by worldwide use of information technology through radio, television and the press;
- a consequent drive towards industrialization as the indispensable means of raising living standards, reducing poverty, becoming 'developed', and coping with the problems of survival which affect four fifths of the human population.

This assemblage of assumptions, practices and aspirations amount to a treadmill to nowhere. But in recognizing it as such, it is still extremely difficult to get off.

We are perhaps the first human generation to see the global effects of the industrial revolution. Even in countries which have most profited from it and thereby achieved unimaginable standards of material wealth, there are growing problems of unsustainability across the whole field of economic activity, including prospects for employment at a time when computers can do more and more work, and of growing inequalities within the system. A good illustration is business behaviour as the economy moves out of recession. Who is taking on more permanent labour? Efficiency has come to mean downsizing without regard to the longer term social consequences.

Yet who can find a politician or other leader who does not still talk of economic growth, full employment and application of market forces as answers to problems which affect ordinary people the world over?

Fortunately for future generations, this culture is already changing. Over the last twenty-five years there has been growing anxiety about the magnitude of the dangers it presents not only to humans but to the ecosystems of life of which humans are a small part:

- the period between the Stockholm Conference in 1972 and the Rio Conference in 1992 marked a substantial change in human attitudes towards the environment. Who could have imagined in 1972 that twenty years later there would be conventions on climate change, biodiversity, and an agreed compendium of environmental requirements for the twenty-first century?
- Correspondingly there are the beginnings of understanding of the need for change in human aspirations: away from crude and

unrealizable aims of ever-increasing Western-type material prosperity towards notions of a relatively steady state society in balance with the Earth's resources and environment.

● likewise there is a new sense of the practical possibilities of what people and their governments can do to move from where we are to where we want to be through use of the means and instruments at our command. Over time we can put at least some things right if we have the will to do so.

There can be nothing more difficult than changing underlying assumptions. As was well said by David Orr, 'looking ahead to the 21st century, the task of building a sustainable world order will require dismantling the jerry built scaffolding of ideas, philosophies and ideologies that constitute the modern curriculum'. Obviously education, and the values implicit in education, constitute the key.

Education

In simple terms the aim must be to produce citizens able to develop their potentialities both as individuals and members of the community, to live in reasonable harmony with their surroundings, to think for themselves, and to cope with problems as we can now foresee them.

At the root of education for sustainability is the notion of interconnectedness. All the issues I have already outlined lead into each other, and cannot be dealt with in isolation. In most discussions of the curriculum, people put environment into the box labelled science, or the box labelled geography, or the box labelled biology, or in some cases the box labelled technology. But the environment is equally relevant to the boxes labelled economics, history, sociology, politics, and all except the most extreme specializations. Environment reaches right across the board. It needs those with a capacity for synthesis, perhaps philosophers, to establish the connections.

This is sometimes labelled multi-disciplinary activity. But that too gives a misleading impression. Of course it is multi-disciplinary. But more important, it is interdisciplinary. It represents complex linkages between disciplines, and the dynamic relationships between them. It means seeing different problems in terms of each other.

This involves an assault on what some regard as the glory and others the bane of the British educational system: specialization. There is a remarkable trend, beginning, as I remember myself, when students are thirteen or fourteen, and reaching through to post-graduate research at universities, whereby they learn more and more about less and less. It should be no surprise that the human results should sometimes be so lopsided, that the notorious gap between the arts and the sciences should be as deep as ever (with those on each side looking disdainfully upon the other), and that the idea of education and re-education as a continuous process throughout life should have had so little resonance in this country.

Inter-connectedness between and across disciplines engenders a dynamic approach towards learning that encourages independent thinking. It also accommodates necessary notions of uncertainty. Learning cannot be static. When I look at the areas with which I am best acquainted - say climate, biodiversity, history, and even astronomy - I find that facts and their interpretation are in constant movement.

This brings me to the most vexed and difficult question of all: values. No system of education anywhere is without values, implicit or explicit, or at least priorities. It is a dangerous illusion to think otherwise. I remember that in recent discussion about geography in the core curriculum, the Department for Education demanded a course full of facts rather than judgements on them. But the selection of facts is itself a judgement, and teaching of geography, like anything else, involves judgement all the time.

Of course we inherit the intellectual baggage of our parents, their social background, the prevailing culture, and the other standards of the society in which we live. Perhaps the most important thing teachers can do is to lead their students into thinking about values themselves, to learn how to challenge as well as accept them, to point out the weaknesses in argument or logical gaps, to inculcate the means by which values can be judged and to give them confidence in themselves. With the current decline in religious belief and practice has come a relativity in values. For many tolerance means acceptance of almost any old values. But even if values today are not those handed down from on high in sacred books, and values are seen as social artefacts, some are nevertheless much better than others. It is the job of teachers to enable students to work through them, argue them out, and achieve a workable result. It is the job of philosophers, acting as building inspectors, to test the reliability, internal consistency and viability of intellectual constructions.

There are three other points important in any consideration of values:

- our current system is based on competition in pursuit of material rewards and personal prestige. But competition is incomplete. In many ways notions of competition derive from Charles Darwin's identification of natural selection, and what Herbert Spencer described as survival of the fittest. But this leaves out the equally important notion of co-operation between organisms and the resulting symbiosis within species and ecosystems. The same applies to ourselves. Co-operation and mutual help are just as important as competition and hierarchy;
- education is not confined to classrooms, lecture halls and libraries. It should stretch far beyond. It is hard to understand geography without direct experience of place. History is in stones as well as books. Biology can be learned in meadows, rubbish dumps and the seashore as well as in the laboratory. Astronomy is meaningless without vision of the stars. Students need to open their minds to the world around them in all its complexity if they are to shed illusions about human domination of nature and the technological fix;
- the one big difference a visitor would notice in classrooms today by comparison with those of thirty years ago is the introduction of computers and computer technology. This must be welcome. - Modelling has greatly enlarged human understanding, and computer literacy from early years is a prize. But there are dangers. T.H. Huxley once wrote:

'Mathematics may be compared to a mill of exquisite workmanship, which grinds you stuff of any degree of fineness; but nevertheless what you get out depends upon what you put in; and as the grandest mill in the world will not extract wheatflour from peascod, so pages of formulae will not get a definite result out of loose data.'

In other words garbage in, garbage out. Here again the philosophers are essential. We have all seen the erection of pagodas of thought, often based on incomplete information and thus wonky modelling, which collapse when subjected to realistic analysis. We need always to regard technology as a means rather than an end, and keep its use in balance with the wider objectives of education. As George Orwell once remarked: the logical end of technological progress is 'to reduce the human being to something resembling a brain in a bottle'.

The System

At last there is better realization of the importance of nursery and primary education. In this the environment has a central place. In many ways children below the age of thirteen, and still more below the age of seven, understand environmental issues and take them more to heart than do grown-ups. They see the world as it is and not through a distorting prism. At the recent meeting of the British Association, Noel Sheehy pointed out that they have a surprising grasp of systems of thought: conservation, erosion, extinction, greenhouse effect, pollution and recycling. Their sense of animism also helps.

'... Many six year olds have no difficulties with the idea that Father Christmas can within twenty four hours circumnavigate the planet with a team of flying reindeer. Some believe in leprechauns and in the fairies at the bottom of the garden. A mind capable of accommodating these ideas will have no difficulty at all with anything that environmental science might offer.'

Perhaps it is the teachers who have to broaden their minds.

Big psychological changes take place at puberty. Children are beginning to adjust to the adult world, and the apparatus of this world is increasingly imposed on them. Examination requirements loom larger and larger, and learning becomes fragmented with corresponding loss of the interconnectedness which was so evident earlier. But a good deal, nourished by interest in the media and elsewhere, remains. At a recent meeting with teachers from a large independent school, I learned that discussion of the environment was largely driven by pupil-power. Teachers responded rather than led. This was not for lack of interest on the part of the teachers, but rather of their awareness of the tight requirements of the examination system.

The contents and character of the new core curriculum are obviously crucial. The aims, recently stated by the Department for Education, seem excellent. They are to:

- 'Provide all pupils with opportunities to acquire the knowledge, understanding and skills required to engage effectively with environmental issues;
- Encourage pupils to examine and interpret the environment from a variety of perspectives - physical, geographical, biological, sociological, economic, political, technological, historical, aesthetic, ethical and spiritual;
- Arouse pupils' awareness and curiosity about the environment, and encourage active participation in resolving environmental problems.'

The problem is how to do it.

Perhaps the first point is that environmental teaching should come in one way or another into virtually all aspects of the curriculum. So far it is mandatory only in the narrow range of geography, science and technology. There are also three important omissions. Nowhere is there recognition of the inter-connectedness of environmental issues and the complexities of their relationships; nor of the need for pupils to be able to integrate the perspectives gained from different disciplines into a coherent view of the world; nor of the place for consideration of environmental values. Such issues should fall naturally into philosophy, ethics, religion, and community rights and obligations.

Even to meet the objectives laid down by the Department for Education will require re-teaching of the teachers. Guidance is needed on how they should take advantage of the knowledge, materials and help from local communities and environmental organisations. There is also need for guidance about how best to use the discretionary time available.

This in turn will require re-examination of examinations. I have long thought that the A-level system as now constituted is indefensible. So long as it exists, it distorts educational priorities within the schools, and it contributes to distortion of priorities within the universities.

So far most - but not all - universities have yet to come to terms with the environment and environmental teaching, particularly at undergraduate level. The report of the Toyne Commission, published in February 1993, brought out the main issues. It drew attention to three main strands of environmental education at this level: specialist courses leading to academic or vocational qualifications; courses on environmental topics for people already in employment; and cross-curricular greening (or action to increase environmental literacy amongst the student body as a whole).

So far the Department for Education has done little more than circulate copies of the report to interested parties. It has taken the view that the Department has no powers to intervene, and that the twenty-eight recommendations in the report should be dealt with by those directly concerned, in particular the Funding Councils.

Abroad, and in particular in the United States, things are different. In October 1990 there was a meeting of twenty-two presidents, rectors and vice-chancellors of universities from all over the world at the European Center of Tufts University in Talloires in France. The result was a report and statement entitled University Presidents for a Sustainable Future: the Talloires Declaration. Since then the Declaration has been endorsed by more than two hundred heads of universities from over forty countries. It concluded with ten points for action. They covered three main areas: interdisciplinary work; internal environmental management; and cooperation with institutions, business, industry and the public generally in moving towards an environmentally sustainable future.

Declarations are one thing, and action on them is another. So far results are patchy. Some British universities are already moving in the same direction, albeit at different speeds, but so far as I know, only one or two British universities have endorsed it. In this country we have a lot to learn from what has been achieved at such American universities as Tufts and Brown.

Universities are a unique resource for teaching and research, but they are not the whole story. The last year of a student's university life is often spent in looking for jobs. To judge from the experience of Brown University, the number of specialized jobs in the environmental field is steadily increasing. But there needs to be better cooperation between employers and educational establishments in designing courses. More important understanding of the environmental dimension in all jobs is already increasing. The greening of human values through education would be of little avail if there were not a corresponding greening of society, government, business and the rest at the same time. Slowly but visibly this is beginning to happen.

There is a lead from the top: governments have entered into a range of international obligations which require real changes in economic management (for example the reduction of carbon emissions to 1990 levels by 2000). Within Britain there is new and tough legislation on environmental issues, and the Bill to constitute an Environment Agency is passing through Parliament. At the same time such bodies as the Advisory Council on Business in the Environment, the International Chambers of Commerce, and the World Business Council for Sustainable Development are in their different ways bringing the environmental dimension into business and industry. Let us hope that the professions - lawyers, bankers, chartered accountants, doctors - are doing likewise.

The Government has just published the second in a series of reports entitled *This Common Inheritance*. Last year it set up a Government Panel on Sustainable Development to advise the government on the issues raised in its paper and monitor its progress across the environmental field. The role of the environment in education was one of the topics selected for study, and was a subject of the Panel's annual report published in January. Since then there has been a full day conference attended by the Secretaries of State for Education and of the Environment, and last week the Government published its response to the Panel's recommendations. The nub was that over the summer the Government would 'be reviewing its overall approach to education, training and awareness-raising about the environment with a view to seizing precisely the kind of coherent and comprehensive approach that the Panel recommends'. The subject is already on the agenda of the new Round Table for Sustainable Development and will be taken up within the Government's initiative at local level known as Going for Green.

In some ways Scotland is ahead of the rest of the United Kingdom. A report entitled *Learning for Life* was commissioned by the Scottish Secretary and published in April 1993. It sets out a ten year strategy which we could all, the Scots included, do well to follow.

I have ranged widely from sustainability to education by way of values and the greening of society. This is an enormous agenda. For those who encounter resistance, whether from sophistry or vested interest, I have a two-edged word of encouragement. Nature will surely win in the end. The question is when and how? After more damage to our society, to life in general, and to the good health of the planet? Or in conformity with a redirection of human thought and endeavour? In my view it would be as well to be on the winning side from the start.

Education towards a partnership with Nature

Andreas Suchantke

The title of this article may strike most readers as illusory given that all over the world the opposite trend dominates, with ruthless exploitation and destruction on such a scale that all well-intended conservation measures must fail. One result of this is resignation and demoralization. The results of the Rio Conference or the Climate Summit in Berlin reveal that nothing serious is undertaken and that all the protestations are really cosmetic sound-bites. We can add to this, indifference and the fact that we have long since got used to shocking announcements about acid rain or the destruction of the ozone layer.

This is one side of the issue, perhaps the adult side. On the other side there is the inner and often the outer, active involvement of many young people in conservation organisations and ecological initiatives. A majority of young people, when asked which institution they found most plausible and worthy, listed Greenpeace in first place (followed significantly by Amnesty International). They rated traditional institutions, usually considered responsible, such as governments, political parties, trades unions, etc., at the bottom of the scale. A study made in German schools gave a similar result. 70% - 80% of the pupils, as against only 50% of the teachers, found themselves called upon to do something about environmental problems. Not only that, but the students were far more willing to accept limitations than adults. (Kasek and Lehwald 1991)

These and other studies, which can be confirmed by regular contact with adolescents, show that there has been a significant shift in consciousness amongst young people who feel moved by what mankind does to Nature, animals, plants and native environments, such as tropical rain forests. This can be seen in active conservation programmes and even in the creation of legislation as well as in the role model function of Greenpeace, WWF and other similarly orientated organisations. The trend is to protect living beings, not in order to maintain or improve the life quality of people, but for their own sakes. This ecocentric approach, which is to be clearly distinguished from anthropocentric motivations, shows many significant parallels to the social renewal and reform movements of the 19th and early 20th centuries (Suchantke 1993).

So-called 'realists' tend to see an unworldly idealism in these ecocentric endeavours and reject or attack them as antiprogressive. They overlook, however, the fact that a merely anthropocentric environmental conservation does not, on its own help, since it concerns itself primarily with restorative measures and technical improvements (e.g. better controls on atomic power stations). Such measures only tackle symptoms and not causes. They neglect the fact that human life quality can only be sustained when nature is healthy and that this can only be achieved when not only our own, but also the life quality of Nature is respected and guaranteed. Environmental conservation which is only anthropocentric is doomed to failure; its necessary complement is an ecocentric approach to Nature.

This is, of course, common knowledge. Its implementation, however, is opposed by a curious modern assumption that is not only widespread in ecological or environmental circles. According to this view the human being is generally fated to be aggressive and destructive. This is the result of extreme living conditions during the Pliocene which led to the selection of traits linked to the ability to prevail, in other words, to be aggressive, becoming part of our genetic inheritance. What then was an advantage has, according to this view, become a disadvantage in a changed environment, where tolerance and peaceful behaviour are required.

An extensive literature on this theme has sought to prove that the evolution of mankind since the appearance of Homo sapiens has been an uninterrupted story of extermination and destruction. (Mosimann and Martin 1967, Crosby 1988). Interestingly, many of these presentations don't bear closer scrutiny (compare Rothausen 1979), especially those written by biologists, who often lack the necessary cultural-historical knowledge (see 'cultureless picture of the human being in Biology' by Gropengiesser and

Kauffman 1991). Such ideas often prove to be projections of contemporary pessimism (specifically by representations of western industrialized nations), rather than objective reality. They are popular because they confirm what has long been suspected.

Thus follows a fatal conclusion. The logical consequence is therefore, from an ecocentre point of view, that there is only one solution to the conservation of nature; the separation of nature from culture.

This leads to attempts to protect Nature by the exclusion of people. In place of confrontation we put separation. That protection of Nature is necessary cannot be denied, on the contrary. Only it is totally useless if destructive activities are carried on in the neighbouring areas. Air pollution or the build-up of pesticide levels can't in the end be kept out. Without a significantly more comprehensive consideration of the life-conditions of Nature, which in the end serves our own needs, we can't go on like this much longer.

So we do need partnership after all. But how? A differentiated analysis of the interdependent relationship of people and Nature can in fact show us ways. More exact studies show the claim that mankind has an exclusively destructive relationship to Nature to be scientifically untenable. They can be briefly summarized here since they are eminently germane to the theme of this article.

We can recognise distinct phases in the development of cultures all over the world, though certainly not all cultures pass through them all. Many communities remain at an earlier stage, notably the hunters and gatherers. They are particularly characterized by the fact that they hardly alter the environments in which they live. They adapt themselves to their environment in a remarkable way without altering the natural balance, much as plants and animals do. Their animalistic consciousness is directed to fitting into their environment and they respect the forces of nature which they experience as authorities.(see Hallpike 1979)

At the next stage this is quite different, namely at the stage of agriculture, which developed in different regions of the world quite independently. Now the transformation of the natural ecosystem begins. This development always begins with a destruction of the natural balance - a good example being the extensive forest clearances in the setting of Europe. It is decisive, however, that it does not remain a destruction.

In place of a natural environment a cultural landscape is created, which is by no means less rich. The creation of a poorer landscape has only been achieved by modern, highly technical agriculture. On the contrary, through small scale, richly diverse cultures and often extensive but careful cultivation it is possible for large numbers of wild plants and species to inhabit the newly created landscape. We know that a large number of plants and animals followed the extension of agriculture into Europe (see *Figure 1* and Pott 1988, Suchantke 1993). An unexpected enrichment of flora and fauna is the consequence of the creation of new environments by mankind. Indeed new species arise. In this way mankind provides Nature with a new evolutionary impulse. (Landolt 1970, Sukopp 1972,1978). The contrast to modern agriculture which has become the leading destroyer of species, couldn't be greater. The vast majority of plant and animal species on the endangered list or which have become extinct, are native to cultivated landscapes.

It is significant that this kind of agriculture which developed in the High Middle Ages was far from unproductive. New technological developments and better farming methods led to a real 'agricultural revolution' (see White 1968) which meant a significant reduction in famine and a notable growth in population.

The decline began in the next phase of development, the transition to urban culture, a process which took place at different times in different regions of the world. The degradation of the landscape began in the Mediterranean regions during the period of ancient Greece and Rome; in Central and Western Europe the decline started with the Renaissance and coincided with the enormous expansion of towns and cities. The world of work of the town dweller is fundamentally different to that of the farmer. In place of the careful way with plants and animals, which is necessary for them to be productive for human needs, man began to work with dead substance. It now depended on the intelligence, the activity and the ingenuity of the individual, as to what could be developed out of it. A rapid development of technology occurred. The first science, physics, developed out of craftwork and with it began the mastery of the 'dead' inorganic nature. The human beings experienced themselves no longer as partner but as master

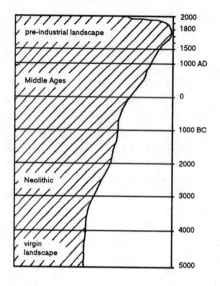

Figure 1. Increase in species diversity of wild plants during the transition from natural to cultivated landscape and the drastic reduction in recent years. (After Sukopp 1972)

of nature: 'man must force nature to obey' (Francis Bacon, in *Novum Organon*, 1620).

The application of causal analytical methods learned from the inorganic realm, on living organisms brought, and still brings today great success, but also in increasing scale, unexpected consequences and side-effects since in living systems everything is functionally linked to and interrelates with everything else. Many increasingly intractable problems today, such as the resistance of pests and harmful organisms have to do with this. Such problems call more and more on ecology which researches such relationships in the expectation that this science can provide better ways of working.

It is not possible here to describe in detail the historical change in the relationship between human beings and Nature. The reference to it here is however crucial since this aspect of history has been relegated to a peripheral role in the History of Science, from which it has had no influence over what is taught in schools.

It is no longer possible to go on teaching history in the way it has been popularized in an exclusively anthropocentric way in which the changing relationship between people and nature has been as good as ignored. The didactic significance of this addition to history teaching hardly needs to be emphasized. Not only could it present a truer picture but it could go a long way to counteracting the widespread sense of resignation and could correct the exclusively negative picture of the destructive side of human nature. It would encourage young people, because it could show that the human being is quite capable of entering into partnership with Nature, if he or she wants to.

Even this, however, is not enough. Reaching nostalgically to past times is also insufficient. Working in partnership with nature also exists today, particularly in two areas which are not only relevant to the present but point the way to the future.

On the one hand we find a dwindling number of original cultures in various parts of the world. The dominant and unforgivable attitude of Colonialism and Neo-colonialism that expresses itself in the mishandling or simply ignoring of so-called 'primitive' cultures and which has long sought to transform the whole world into a kind of 'Neo Europe'(Crosby 1988), is guilty of enormous ecological damage in Third World countries. The classic example are the rainforests which in the view of many experts are not suitable for agriculture because of their leached and sterile soils and which because of their eminent ecological significance and their role as gene reservoirs are to be put under total protection. In reality, as we know, the opposite is true. Irresponsible logging and burning threaten the existence of the rain forests altogether.

In fact there is a viable solution to the problem. The possibility of using the tropical forests as an agricultural resource whilst preserving them, is not only theory but has been practised successfully for a long time. The trouble is we haven't noticed - for the simple reason that nobody was really interested in the 'primitive' peoples who live in these forests. Ethno-ecological research over the past few decades has produced an outstanding catalogue of facts showing that some of the Amazonian rain forest tribes have developed highly differentiated methods of agro-forestry that make productive use of the forests as well as fully preserving the bio-diversity of the environment. (Porey 1983, Brose 1988, Suchantke 1993).

Large areas of apparently natural rain-forest in the Yucatan (Mexico) were revealed to have been planted by people and offered in the pre-Spanish times living opportunities for a higher population density than it now supports. (Gomez-Pompa and Kaus 1990).

The techniques applied there and the accumulated experience could immediately be taken up, and the apparently hopeless situation of the rain forests could be relieved. Apart from which, large numbers of uprooted people that now eke out an existence in the city slums could be resettled there with the possibility of a humanly worthy basis for life.

This is also a subject which should be taught in school, and for two reasons. Firstly, in an age of encounter and often confrontation between different cultures, it is vital that such encounters do not remain of a superficial nature which remains at the level of strangers and can lead to mutual rejection. Rather the inner values and achievements of other cultures should be discovered and appreciated. On the other hand, there is hardly anything interests many youngsters more passionately than the fate of the rainforests. It is a theme that can become a focus of hope for change in our dealings with nature. The author regularly experiences in conversation with young people and school classes how quickly an emerging sense of resignation can change into enthusiasm when one reports on this ethno-ecological research and of the achievement of say, the Kayapó-Indios of the Brazilian Rain Forest.

The approach to changes in modern agricultural methods has to be of a very practical nature. Modern agriculture is highly technical and dependent on many agro-chemicals and it is becoming apparent that in view of the environmental damage and health risks that it causes, such as the pollution of drinking water and the increase of pesticide levels in food products, things must change. Increasing numbers of farmers are becoming willing to change to environmentally friendly methods based on ecological understanding. This is also a way of moving away from economically senseless over-production and the degradation of the landscape through monoculture. The trend towards an integration of varied cultivation methods and towards a combination of arable farming and animal husbandry will lead towards a new agricultural landscape; one which is more varied, richly differentiated and nearer to Nature. Similarly, forestry is increasingly moving away from monoculture plantations which limit the growth of compatible vegetation and towards more natural self-regenerating mixed woods. Even if these trends are still modest beginnings, they nevertheless are indications of a revival of methods given up in the late Middle Ages, but which can be taken up in a modern way suitable to the demands of our times.

Here we have the opportunity of leading school lessons out of the merely theoretical into a practical approach. In Steiner-Waldorf Schools the particular care and cultivation of plants, in various ways appropriate to the age of the child, is taught through practical experience from the Kindergarten to the upper classes. In the upper classes, in which a social practical is part of each year's curriculum, a 3-4 week work-experience block is usually carried out on a ecologically oriented farm. Thus theory is complemented by intensive practice. In this way the tendency current today of being well informed as to what needs doing but unable to do anything about it, can be counterbalanced. Rudolf Steiner justified the introduction of gardening lessons into the Waldorf School (founded in 1919) as follows:

> 'People who have had this experience in school, are then in a position to judge whether a particular method or practice in agriculture is right or not, not because they have learned it, but because they have gained a certainty of feeling about it. Moral qualities are also exercised in such lessons. The consequences of such lessons will lie in the social attitude of the adult.'

These words anticipated the crisis in modern agriculture and at the same time suggested a way to a solution. Agriculture has long posed a question to the whole of society and in the end it is the attitude of the consumer which will determine the nature of the solution. Ignorance and apathy, however, hinder any influence they may have. This would be changed as soon as gardening lessons and farming work-experience opportunities became a part of general school education. Steiner's intentions for these lessons were not aimed at training future gardeners or farmers but to cultivate a 'certainty of feeling' in the pupils. Anyone who has spent time intensively at a certain activity will gain on the one hand the 'right feeling' for whichever method is appropriate or not, and on the other hand, if it is done correctly, one becomes connected to a given complex of problems. One becomes involved and it is this which Steiner meant by 'moral qualities or forces' (Suchantke 1995).

Practical experience weds itself to knowledge and understanding. What is also necessary is the engagement of the emotions through which arise a sense of connection, of interest and ultimately of love. A feeling of love towards Nature, and naturally towards people, forms the foundation on which everything else can be built, or rather that element which penetrates both intellectual and practical activity. Out of this can grow the ethical motivation, self-sustaining, encouraging, and supporting the will to tackle problems. The experiences of disappointment with merely scientific environmental studies in school that we mentioned at the beginning of this article speak for themselves. Merely preaching ethics is worthless. What must develop is an ethic of the heart.

As we have seen this can be found in childhood and youth to a forceful extent. It is especially true of the pre-school and early school age. The child's consciousness differs from that of the adult in that there is no separation between self and environment, there is as yet no alienation. As Jean Piaget's research has shown, for the young child, there is as yet no world of things. What the adult experiences as objects, are for the child subjects, feeling, living beings, but not things: the moon and the sun, the flowers are, in the experience of the child, beings like him or herself. If we go for a walk with a child on a moonlit night the moon comes along too - why? Because the moon wants to know where the child is going! If the moon hides for a moment behind a cloud then it is because it is tired and wants to rest (Piaget 1926).

As this example shows, the child's animalistic consciousness is so formed that everything orientates itself and directs itself towards the child. It is a complete, familiar and related world - not a world around me - an environment - but a world within which one is. In such a participatory world plants or the moon behave like the child him or herself. A single flower in a vase may be lonely and need the company of a few grasses as friends from the same meadow.

This example reveals another characteristic of the young child's consciousness. What is decisive is not the sense-perceptible object, but the related soul experience of the child which is on the one hand strongly determined by feeling and on the other hand possesses the character of an imaginative mental image which complements the sense-perception of the object itself. Anyone can experience this in telling a child a story or fairytale. The strength of this inner picturing can be read in the intensity of the child's accompanying reactions - as the child pales, or holds its breath in fearful tension, then laughs in happy release. It is not easy to adequately name this kind of child experience, since the concepts we have available are drawn from adult experience. 'Picture' or 'mental picturing' already possess the character of something outside of us that we look upon from our standpoint. The child, however, stands within the picture.

If we wish to bring the child closer to Nature at this age then we must not force the child out of its world of experience and confront it with the specific otherness of the things of the world. This process of standing back from the world, which is the beginning of an alienation necessary to the experience of the other as something different, occurs naturally in the child between the age of 8 and 10 (Piaget). At this age the ability of operational and generalized thinking awakens. If this occurs too early then the child is torn out of its place in the familiar world to which he or she instinctively feels it belongs and is cast into an unhealthy alienation.

The very opposite is necessary. The objects and things must be brought into this familiar world and imbued with the emotionally rich picture - quality that characterizes the child's consciousness. Rachel Carson, author of the famous book *'Silent Spring'*, described this in a masterful way. In her late years she had to look after her orphaned nephew Roger:

'Having always loved the lichens because they have a quality of fairyland - silver rings on a stone. Odd little forms like bones or horns or the shell of a sea creature - I was glad to find Roger noticing and responding to the magic change in their appearance wrought by the rain. The wood's path was carpeted with the so-called reindeer moss, in reality lichen. Like an old-fashioned hall runner, it made a narrow strip of silvery gray through the green of the woods, here and there spreading out to cover a larger area. In dry weather the lichen carpet seems thin; it is brittle and crumbles underfoot. Now, saturated with rain which it absorbs like a sponge, it was deep and springy. Roger, delighted in its texture, getting down on chubby knees to feel it, and running from one patch to another to jump up and down in the deep, resilient carpet with squeals of pleasure.

It was here that we first played our Christmas tree game, there is a fine crop of young spruces coming along and one can find seedlings of almost any size down to the length of Roger's finger. I began to point out the baby trees.

"This one must be a Christmas tree for the squirrels, I would say. It's just the right height. On Christmas Eve the red squirrels come and hang little shells and cones and silver threads of lichen on it for ornaments, and then the snow falls and covers it with shining stars, and in the morning the squirrels have a beautiful Christmas tree...And this one is even tinier - it must be for little bugs of some kind - and maybe this bigger one is for the rabbits or woodchicks."

Once this game was started it had to be played on all woods walks, which from now on were punctuated by shouts of "Don't step on the Christmas tree."'

This example points to one other aspect, namely the emphasis on the sense experience of the child. The child is incomparably more open, and at the same time defenceless, against its environment than the adult. The way Roger unites himself with all his senses with his environment and almost becomes bodily at one with it, is the physical correlation to the psychological emotion of oneness. Here we see the decisive opportunity to lead the child to nature and to unite nature permanently with the way of experience of the child. The fact that Nature in so doing may be made anthropomorphic from an adult point of view need not be damaging. The alienation that naturally comes about at a later stage will gradually replace an 'animalistic' way of seeing with scientific concepts. What remains, however, is the emotional bonding, the sense of familiarity, the affection and the love, all of which provide an ethical foundation.

The example from Rachel Carson shows how the child's experience is based on two supports; on the one hand the child's own emphasis on sensory experience and the ability to experience sense-impressions so intensively that this forms the primary mode of learning in early childhood - namely through imitation through the sense organs.

On the other hand the child experiences the world through the emotionally felt, pictorial images, the meaning of which the child continuously demands of the adult world, parents, kindergarten teachers and so on. How this inner world of pictures is structured and what meaning it possesses is in the hands of adults. If this psychological nourishment is neglected, then there is the risk of an inner poverty of experience which can lead more and more to a closing off of the senses in forms of autism.

There is nothing that offers a richer, more differentiated field of experiences and impressions than Nature with all her colours, forms, movements, sounds, smells and tactile qualities. Here lies the source for a permanent inner wealth for the human being - assuming, of course, that it has been accompanied in the right way by adults who have imbued the experience with meaningful content. The stories we tell do not have to possess literary merit. It is enough if the adults themselves experience something real and shares these experiences with the child. A robin redbreast 'babbles like a silver brook' or a thrush greets the sunrise.

The important thing, however, is how stories are told and what content they are given. The shadow picture to Rachel Carson's approach is represented by the picture world of Walt Disney who brilliantly understood how to reach (and market) the child's world of experience. The incredible success of Mickey Mouse proves how accurately he discovered the child's soul. More problematical, however, is the ethical side of Disney's picture stories in which sentimentality, malicious or vicarious pleasure, deception or cunning often triumph.

As Rachel Carson puts it:

> 'If a child is to keep alive his inborn sense of wonder he needs the companionship of at least one adult who can share it, rediscovering with him the joy, excitement and mystery of the world we live in. Parents often have a sense of inadequacy...'

"How can I possibly teach my child about nature - why, I don't know one bird from another."
I sincerely believe that for the child, and for the parent seeking to guide him, it is not half so important to **know** as to **feel**. If facts are the seeds that later produce knowledge and wisdom, then the emotions and the impressions of the senses are the fertile soil in which the seeds must grow. The years of early childhood are the time to prepare the soil. Once the emotions have been aroused - a sense of the beautiful, the excitement of the new and the unknown, a feeling of sympathy, pity, admiration or love - then we wish for knowledge about the object of our emotional response. Once found, it has lasting meaning. It is more important to pave the way for the child to want to know than to put him on a diet of facts he is not ready to assimilate.' (Rachel Carson)

Translated by Martyn Rawson

References

Bacon, F. (1620): *Novum Organon*
Brose, M. (1988): *Vielfalt als Grundkonzept standortgerechten Landbaues in Zentralbrasilien.* Lateinamerika - Dokumentationstelle FB 6, Gesamthochschule Kassel.
Carson, R. (1965): *A Sense of Wonder.* New York.
Crosby, A.W. (1988): *Exological Imperialism. The Biological Expansion of Europe, 900 - 1900.* Cambridge.
Hallpike, C.R. (1979): *The Foundations of Primitive Thought.* Oxford.
Kasek, I., Lehwald, G. (1991): *Umweltbefragung Schüler Lehrer Eltern.* Umweltinstitut Leipzig, Bereich Sozialökologie.
Landolt, I. (1970): *Mitteleuropäische Wiesenpflanzen als hybridogene Abkömmlinge von mittel- und südeuropäischen Gebirgssippen.* Feddes Repertorium 81: 61-66.
Mosimann, K.E., Martin, P.S. (1967): *Pleistocene Extinctions. The Search for a Cause.* New Haven.
Piaget, J. (1926): *La représentation du monde chez l'enfant.* Paris.
Posey, D.A. (1983): *Indigenous knowledge and development of the Amazon,* in D.A. Moran (Ed); the dilemma of American Development. Boulder.

Co. (1983) *Indigenous knowledge and development: an ideological bridge to the future.* Ciência e Cultura 35. No. 7: 877 - 894.

Pott, R. (1988): *Entstehung von Vegetationstypen und Pflanzengesellschaften unter dem Einfluß des Menschen.* Düsseldorfer Geobotanische Kolloquien 5.

Rothausen, K. (1972), *Literaturbesprechung,* in Zentralblatt für Geologie und Paläontologie Teil II: Paläontologie Jahrgang 1970: 78 - 81.

Suchantke, A. (1993): *Partnerschaft mit der Natur. Entscheidung für das kommende Jahrtausend. Stuttgart.. (1995): Der umweltpädagogische Ansatz der Waldorfpädagogik.* Erziehungskunst, Themenheft Umwelterziehung. April 1995: 338 - 349.

Sukopp, H. (1972): *Wandel von Flora and Vegetation in Mitteleuropa unter dem Einfluß des Menschen.* Ber. Landwirtschaft 50: 112 - 139. (1978): *Veränderungen von Flora und Vegetation durch den Menschen,* in G. Olschowy (Ed.): Natur- und Umweltschutz in der Bundesrepublik Deutschland. Hamburg - Berlin.

White, L. (1968) *Mittelalterliche Technik und der Wandel der Gesellschaft.* München. Vergleiche auch W. Abel (1978): *Geschichte der deutschen Landwirtschaft vom frühen Mittelalter bis zum 19. Jahrhundert.* Stuttgart).

Appendix I

Private Schools in Denmark: A Framework for a Pluralist, Free Education System?

Reproduced by kind permission of the Danish Ministry of Education and Research, April 1992

Denmark has a tradition of private schools with a substantial government subsidy. This tradition mainly originates in the ideas and initiatives of the clergyman, poet and politician, N.F.S. Grundtvig (1783-1872), and the teacher, Christen Kold (1816-1870). On the basis of their ideas about 'a school for life based on the living word', the first 'folk high school' for adults was founded in 1844, and the first 'free school' (private independent school) for children was founded in 1852. They were in particular meant to serve the rural population.

The ideas of Grundtvig and Kold had such an impact on the political thinking of their time that they were written into the democratic Constitution adopted by Denmark in 1849. It stipulates general compulsory education - not compulsory school attendance.

In Denmark, all children between the age of 7 and 16 must receive education but - provided a certain minimum standard is obtained - it is a matter of choice for the parents whether the education is received

1) in the publicly provided municipal school,
2) in a private school, or
3) at home.

Number of schools and pupils in private schools

About 10% of all children at basic school level (including the voluntary pre-school and 10th form) attend private schools. In 1991, approx. 70,000 children attended 409 private schools, while

540,000 pupils attended the municipal school of which there are approximately 1,800.

Types of schools

Private schools in Denmark may be roughly divided into the following categories:

- small 'Grundtvigian' independent schools in rural districts,
- academically oriented lower secondary schools (the so-called 'réal-schools'),
- religious or congregational schools such as Catholic or Danish Mission schools,
- progressive free schools,
- schools with a particular pedagogical aim, such as the Rudolf Steiner schools,
- German minority schools,
- immigrant schools such as the Muslim schools.

The bottom line is that private schools will be recognized and receive government financing regardless of the ideological, religious, political or ethnic motivation behind the establishment.

Legislation

All parties in the Danish Parliament want legislation ensuring financial support for private schools, partly based on the notion that also the municipal schools will benefit from the experience and competition offered by the private schools.

The legislation contains detailed rules about government financial support but only the most general rules about the educational content. There are for example almost no rules about the Ministry of Education's control of the educational performance of the schools. However, the schools may always come to the Ministry for advice if and when they need it, and the Ministry can take special action if needed.

Educational Content

All that is demanded of private education is that it measures up to that of the municipal schools. The Ministry of Education confers on private schools the right to use the municipal schools' final examination and thereby exercises a form of indirect quality control. However, in principle it is not up to any government authority but to the parents of each private school to check that its performance measures up to the demands of the municipal schools.

It is the parents themselves who must choose a supervisor to check the pupils' level of achievement in Danish, arithmetic, mathematics and English. If the school is found inadequate, the superviser must report it to the municipal school authority who may then assign the children to other schools. Individual parents who are dissatisfied with a private school may move their child to another private school or to a municipal school. The local municipal school must always admit the child.

In extraordinary circumstances, the Ministry of Education may establish special supervision, for example if there is reason to believe that the school teaches Danish so poorly that the children's ability to cope with life in Denmark may be impaired.

A new public grants system

In the spring of 1991, the Danish Parliament passed a new private school act. It introduced a new public grants system for private schools giving them a grant towards the operational expenditures 'per pupil per year' which in principle matches the comparable public expenditures in the municipal schools - less the private school fees paid by the parents. This is to ensure that public expenditures for the private and municipal schools follow the same trend.

Operational grants

In 1992, the average grant towards the operational expenditures per pupil per year amounts to about DKK 22,000 (slightly less than 2,000 pounds sterling) and the average fees paid by the parents amount to DKK 6,000 (approximately 500 pounds sterling).

The actual grant per pupil varies from one school to another depending on 3 factors:

- the size of the school (number of pupils),
- the age distribution of the pupils,
- the seniority of the teachers.

The variation ranges from about DKK 19,000 to DKK 30,000. A large school with comparatively young pupils and comparatively young teachers will get a low grant per pupil per year, while the large grant per pupil goes to the small school with older pupils and teachers.

Small schools have always had higher expenditures per pupil than larger schools, but before the 1991 Act, the difference in grants per pupil to large and small schools had unexpectedly become so great that the large private schools were running into financial difficulties. It was therefore stipulated in the 1991 Act that the Folketing each year must consider the question of redistribution of the grants between the small and the large schools. For 1992, it has fixed a redistribution rate of 1.45 for schools with 50 and 400 pupils, respectively. This means that for every DKK per pupil allocated to the large school, the small school will get 1.45.

Special grants

There are also a number of special grants, such as grants towards expenditures incurred in connection with the teaching of pupils with learning disabilities or other special difficulties. The grants are awarded by the Ministry of Education on the basis of a case-by-case assessment. Another special grant is the additional grant received by the German minority schools because they teach in two languages.

Building grants

Until now, schools have received grants towards concrete expenditures in relation to taxes and rates, rent maintenance and construction. As from 1993, they will in principle receive a block grant per pupil to cover all these kinds of building-related expenditures. But this new system will be phased in slowly.

Grant conditions

To be eligible for public financial support, schools must be of a certain minimum size. The 1991 Act requires a school to have a total of at least 28 pupils in the 1st to 7th forms, though only 12 in the school's first year and 20 in its second year.

Furthermore, the school must be a self-governing institution with a board of governors responsible to the Ministry of Education and with rules regulating the use of any net assets in case of liquidation. A school must not be owned by a private individual or run for private profit.

Schools must be able to find a degree of self-financing. The requirement per pupil at present is approximately DKK 3,000 per year.

Joint municipal financing

Education at basic school level is in principle a municipal task, and the municipalities save expenditures on the pupils attending private schools. They are therefore required to reimburse the government a good deal of the government grant. In 1992, the municipal reimbursement rate is about DKK 15,000 per pupil, corresponding to 68% of the public grant.

Private upper secondary schools

In 1992, the government has proposed an act giving the private upper secondary schools the same public grants system as the private basic schools. There are about 20 such schools, and they cater for 6% of all upper secondary school pupils. They differ from the private basic school in that the content of their teaching is governed by the same rules as those applying to the county schools, the reason being that they both lead to the same final examination, i.e. the upper secondary school leaving examination (the 'studentereksamen').

Private and municipal schools

Number of Pupils

School year	Municipal schools	Private schools	Total	P.c. in free schools
1982/83	696,318	61,618	757,936	8.13
1983/84	674,182	62,962	737,144	8.54
1984/85	657,734	64,774	722,508	8.97
1985/86	642,792	66,372	709,164	9.36
1986/87	629,309	67,075	696,384	9.63
1987/88	608,815	67,087	675,902	9.93
1988/89	587,401	67,529	654,930	10.31
1989/90	567,049	67,039	634,088	10.57
1990/91	549,262	67,360	616,622	10.92
1991/92	536,822	66,130	602,952	10.97

Number of Schools

School year	Municipal schools	Private schools	Total	P.c. in free schools
1982/83	1,916	329	2,245	14.65
1983/84	1,905	351	2,256	15.56
1984/85	1,896	361	2,257	15.99
1985/86	1,885	368	2,253	16.33
1986/87	1,866	379	2,245	16.88
1987/88	1,854	390	2,244	17.38
1988/89	1,839	394	2,233	17.64
1989/90	1,830	403	2,233	18.05
1990/91	1,779	409	2,188	18.69

Address:
International Relations Division,Fredriksholms Kanal 25 D,
DK-1220 Copenhagen K.   FAX (0045) 6261 3911

Further Reference:
The Danish Friskole, 1995, Friskole Office, Prices Havevejll,
DK-5600 Faaborg, Denmark.

Appendix II

British Politicians avoid the question of Freeing Education: how to raise it in your school and community

The following letter was sent on 15th September 1995 to the Political Party education representatives, together with the Danish government briefing paper from Appendix I and an Advance Information form for *Freeing Education.*

To:

Gillian Shephard, MP, Secretary of State for Education and Employment
David Blunkett, MP, Shadow Secretary of State for Education
Don Foster, MP, Liberal Democrat education spokesman.

15 September 1995
Freeing Education: Book Proposal

Enclosed is a Danish government briefing paper on 'private' state funded education in Denmark. I am editing a book called *Freeing Education* for publication in November 1995, and would greatly appreciate your brief responses to the following questions, and your kind permission to use these responses in the book. I am also writing to the other Party education representatives with the same questions:
Do you

1) as an individual and

2) as a Party representative support in principle the right of small schools, religious schools such as Muslim schools (Anglicans,

Methodists, Catholics and Jews already have state supported schools), and schools with a particular pedagogical approach such as Rudolf Steiner Schools, to opt in to the state sector as voluntary aided or grant maintained schools?

3) If so, what conditions would you qualify your agreement with? What conditions would the school have to fulfil?

4) In practice, such schools as two Muslim schools, Oak Hill School in Bristol and Holywood Rudolf Steiner School in County Down have tried unsuccessfully to opt in to grant maintained status. Reasons given include, 'there is already a surplus of school places in our area'(Avon LEA), and with Holywood, DENI wrote that 'your school... cannot be considered for acceptance as a grant aided school unless it can provide clear evidence that it is effectively delivering the minimum requirements of the curriculum as enshrined in legislation.'What practical suggestions do you have for helping such schools in what is called 'the reluctant private sector' acquire state support as in such pluralist educational systems as Germany, Holland and Denmark?

5) As you agree with parental choice, in your view, how might the inclusion of different types of school help achieve this policy goal? What in fact do you mean by parental choice?

6) What in your view would be the advantages and disadvantages of supporting a diverse range of schools within the state sector as in Denmark?

Your responses to these questions will be much appreciated and you are welcome to choose whether you are speaking as an individual, or whether this is Party policy. However, I need these responses by October 21st at the latest, and preferably sooner. Yours Sincerely,

Martin Large, Editor.

The replies were as follows:

(1) Mrs G. Shephard MP, Secretary of State for Education and Employment (from M.P. Woolley)

2 November 1995

Dear Mr Large

FREEING EDUCATION: BOOK PROPOSAL

Thank you for your letter of 15 September to the Secretary of State about the book you are publishing. I am sorry that you did not receive a reply before your deadline. Mrs Shephard was unable to reply directly. You may be aware that policy announcements, among other things, are prevailing upon this Department and a reply by officials has been delayed. Current developments could have a bearing upon our answers to your questions but these developments are unlikely to reach a conclusion for some time yet. Even if it were not for this, although you only asked for 'brief responses', the issues you raised deserved a more extensive reply which would have taken some time for us to prepare.

I see that publication of your book was scheduled for this month, however, if some response to your letter would still be useful please let me know. I wish you every success with the book.

M P Woolley
GM Division

---

17 November 1995

CURRENT GOVERNMENT EDUCATION POLICY.
NEW GM AND VA SCHOOLS

CONTRIBUTION TO 'FREEING EDUCATION' BOOK PROPOSAL

It is open to independent promoters, including those running existing independent schools, to make proposals to the Secretary of State for the establishment of new voluntary-aided or grant-maintained schools, whether or not representing a particlar faith or denomination.

The Secretary of State considers all such proposals on their merits against a number of criteria. These include receiving satisfactory evidence that the proposed school would be able to fulfil the requirements applying to all publicly funded schools - for example, to deliver the National Curriculum, to secure that teachers are suitably qualified, and to ensure that equal opportunities are available to boys and girls.

In addition, the Secretary of State considers the proposals in the light of the contribution the school would make to enhancing the quality, choice and diversity of educational provision in the area; the extent of parental demand for the proposed new school and, given the need to secure a cost-effective use of public money, whether there is a need for new school places in the area. The Secretary of State also takes into account, in the case of a proposed new voluntary-aided school, whether the local education authority supports the proposal and, in the case of a new grant-maintained school, whether there is support from the Funding Agency for Schools.

Information also sent included

(1) Extract from White Paper *Choice and Diversity* (1992)
(2) Note on legal basis of 'Education Otherwise'
(3) Assisted Places Scheme

Comment

The practical reality of Government policy on new GM and VA schools is *to date,* that such schools as Steiner Waldorf, Oak Hill School of Bristol and Muslim schools have had their applications for GM status blocked. Both politicians and officials have set up an obstacle course to avoid setting a precedent. However, a further fax (14.12.95) was received from M. Woolley which indicates that the issue is being considered further:

14 December 1995

Oak Hill proposal is complex and must be considered alongside LEA proposals for a new school. Ministers want to reach a decision on all statutory proposals in shortest time possible but must also ensure all issues are given due attention. Furthermore, this is a new area of policy with no precedents.

As to the two Muslim schools you mentioned - these proposals may have been withdrawn. Ministers have only considered **four** proposals to date. Two were approved (St. Anselm's and Upton Hall in Wirral) and two are still under consideration (Jewish Community day school in Herts. and Oak Hill)

M.P.K. Woolley

---

(2) From David Blunkett, MP, Shadow Education Spokesperson

6 October 1995

Dear Mr Large

Thank you very much for your letter.

I am very sorry that I am unable to participate in this questionnaire.

We are getting them almost weekly now and it is becoming impossible to concentrate on the main job in hand and do constituency work as well as assisting with what are all very worthwhile research projects.

With all good wishes.

Yours sincerely

DAVID BLUNKETT

To David Drew, Prospective Parliamentary Candidate for Stroud (Wrote to David Blunkett to ask a second time for a response)

14 November 1995

Dear David

Thank you very much for your letter of 29th October.

Given your special request to me, I am replying to the outline of the questions raised and I hope this will be satisfactory for Hawthorn Press.

We are very happy to welcome into the public sector schools which feel that they have a part to play and which offer a specialist approach not readily available within the existing framework,

We would, of course, have to lay down certain parameters. Schools would have to adhere to the principles laid out in 'Diversity and Excellence' in relation to equity of funding, admissions policy and accountability',

It would not be our intention to reject applications to join the state system without good cause. However, there are obviously issues relating to the configuration of school places in the area. It would not be possible to spend public money on new facilities coming into the state sector where there are already large numbers of surplus places and/or similar provision in the immediate locality. This is for very simple and practical reasons - namely, that the entry of a school into the system should not threaten the viability and continuance of an existing school.

There is good will from the Labour Front Bench towards schools entering the system but with the provisos outlined above and, of course, taking into account the quality threshold which would have to be reached and which is a normal part of any accreditation for state funding.

We are looking at specialist facilities sympathetically but each case will inevitably have to be judged on its merits.

DAVID BLUNKETT

(3) From Don Foster, MP, Liberal Democrat Education
Spokesman

16th October 1995

Dear Mr Large,

Thank you for your letter regarding the publication of *Freeing
Education.*

Liberal Democrats welcome the establishment of voluntary
schools where there is substantial support for such initiatives
within the local community. The decision as to whether such
provision is viable, however, should rest with the democratically
accountable Local Education Authority in each area. There should
be a final right of appeal to the Secretary of State. The Secretary
of State should, in turn, publish the criteria by which such appeals
will be assessed.

Liberal Democrats do not believe it is equitable to grant
voluntary aided or controlled status to the schools of one religion
or denomination, and not to those of another. The DFEE should
publish clear guidance, after the widest possible consultation, on
what criteria such schools are required to meet to qualify for
support and should apply those criteria uniformly, regardless of
religious denomination. The criteria must include a requirement
that the school meets the agreed National Curriculum.

Liberal Democrats oppose the two tier education service created
by the introduction of Grant Maintained status. We have made
clear our view that GM schools should be returned to the light
touch strategic planning framework of the relevant LEA. We
would, therefore, oppose any school opting in to the state system
through the Grant Maintained status route.

Although Liberal Democrats oppose the Assisted Places
Scheme, we are anxious to see developed, at a local level, policies
which enable co-operation between state and independent school
sectors to mutual benefit. At the time of writing this issue is the
subject of considerable debate both within the party and with
organisations representing the independent school sector.

Since the vast majority of parents have little or no choice about
the school to which they send their children, the prospectus of
'parental choice' offered by the present Government is a false

prospectus. Indeed, in the current 'market system' of education introduced by the Government it is often the schools that choose the pupils. Thus while diversity of school provision in areas where real choices can be made is valuable, Liberal Democrats believe that the more crucial issue is to ensure choice within schools rather than between them.

Yours sincerely,

Don Foster, MP

Conclusions

Readers can make their own conclusions from these responses - however, my own include the following:

1. The Minister and her officials are slow and late in their response, indicating a reluctance to enter specific discussion on these issues. There would **seem** to be openings for precedents, however.

2. The book contains contributions from a wide variety of people including nationally well-known figures. The silence from the Minister herself and the reluctant reply from the Labour Education Spokesman is therefore an indication of a lack of interest in an important debate.

(3) A conclusion from this is that education policy making in England and Wales is 'top-down'. The challenging set of questions posed in *Freeing Education* to enable what Michael Young has called 'a diaspora of free schools' is not on the agenda of Ministers, Shadow Spokesmen, their advisors and their officials. Don Foster MP's careful reply also indicates this.

(4) **One response is for schools, teachers, parents, PTA's, governors, students and community representatives to publicly discuss and debate the options for freeing education in their particular school and area. Such debates and discussions could include local political**

party representatives, so that they can discuss freeing education in an informed, open way.

If schools and groups are interested in this, speakers and information can be obtained via Human Scale Education, 96 Carlingcott, Near Bath, BA2 8AW (01761 433733).

Appendix III

International Declarations and Conventions on the Right to Education and the Freedom of Education

UNITED NATIONS
Universal Declaration of Human Rights (1948)

Article 26
1. Everyone has the right to education.
2. Education shall be directed to the full development of the human personality and the strengthening of respect for human rights and fundamental freedoms.
3. Parents have a prior right to choose the kind of education that shall be given to their children.

UNESCO
Recommendation concerning the status of teachers (1966)

61. The teaching profession should enjoy academic freedom in the discharge of professional duties. Since teachers are particularly qualified to judge the teaching aids and methods most suitable for their pupils, they should be given the essential role in the choice and the adaption of teaching material, the selection of textbooks and the application of teaching methods, within the framework of approved programmes, and with the assistance of the educational authorities.
63. Any systems of inspection or supervision should be designed to encourage and help teachers in the performance of their professional tasks and should be such as not to diminish the freedom, initiative and responsibility of teachers.

COUNCIL OF EUROPE
European Convention for the Protection of Human Rights and Fundamental Freedoms. Protocol I (1952)

Article 2
No person shall be denied the right to education. In the exercise of any functions which it assumes in relation to education and to teaching, the State shall respect the right of parents to ensure such education and teaching is in conformity with their own religious and philosophical convictions.

EUROPEAN COMMUNITY
European Parliament: Resolution on Freedom of Education in the European Community (1984)

1. Every child and young person shall have the right to education and teaching; this includes the right of the child to develop his or her abilities; within the framework of the constitutions common to all the Member States and the legislation based thereon, the parent shall have the right to decide on the type of education and teaching to be given to their children of school age;

6. Freedom of education and teaching shall be guaranteed;

7. Freedom of education and teaching shall include the right to establish a school and provide instruction;

It shall further include the right of parents to select, from among comparable schools, a school in which their children will receive the instruction desired; every child must be offered the possibility of attending a school which gives no precedence to specific religious or philosophical beliefs in its education and teaching;

It cannot be the duty of the State to recommend or give preferential treatment either to denominational schools in general or to schools of a particular denomination, nor can the State give such recommendations or preferential treatment to nondenominational education;

It is the parents' right to choose a school for their children until the latter can do so for themselves; it is the duty of the State to provide the necessary facilities for State or private schools;

9. In accordance with the right to freedom of education, Member States shall be required to provide the financial means whereby this right can be exercised in practice, and to make the necessary public grants to enable schools to carry out their tasks and fulfil their duties under the same conditions as in corresponding State establishments, without discrimination as regards administration, parents, pupils or staff;

Notwithstanding this, however, freely established schools shall be required to make a certain contribution of their own as a token of their own responsibility and as a means of supporting their independent status;

European Parliament: Declaration of Fundamental Rights and Freedoms (1989)

Article 16 (Right to Education)

There shall be freedom in education.

Parents shall have the right to make provision for such education in accordance with their religious and philosophical convictions.

EUROPEAN FORUM FOR FREEDOM IN EDUCATION: Declaration concerning the Human Right to Freedom in Education in Europe (1991)

Historical Background

In Europe there has been a long tradition of Freedom in Education. Influenced by this strong ideal of educational diversity, the European Parliament in its Resolution on Freedom of education (1984) broadened the legal framework of schools: 'It is the parents' right to choose a school for their children until the latter can do so for themselves; it is the duty of the State to provide the necessary facilities for State or private schools.' In this the European Parliament confirms the article on parental rights which is set out in the General Declaration of Human Rights (1948) as well as the right of each person to education and to the freedom to set up and run schools which is embedded in the 'International

Covenant on Economic, Social and Cultural Rights' (1966). Furthermore, the concluding document of the Vienna meeting of the Conference on Security and Co-operation in Europe (1989) ensures the right of access to education independent of 'race, colour, sex, language, religion, political or other opinion, national or social origin, property, birth or other status.'

Aims

We are resolved that the basic human right to freedom in education shall become an integral feature of the school landscape in Europe, and we wish to further principles of self-determination which have not yet been realized. The child's right to the free development of personality is a part of schooling, and the human rights movement should not halt at the school door. Freedom in education is just as much a human right as freedom in religion, science, art and the press.

The Place of Education in Society

We are resolved to free schools from State domination and to help them to become centres of cultural life. The imposition of expertise and directives from the State, however well-intentioned, is inappropriate in the field of education. The notion of centralized direction was nowhere so prevalent as in the political systems of Fascism and Communism. Today it must be possible for a variety of educational approaches to co-exist which are carried by the personal initiative of individual parents, teachers and pupils. In these live the creative capacities which not only sustain cultural life but actually bring it into being.

Educational Diversity

We stand for diversity of all viable types of schools which offer equality of opportunity and conform to the rights of children - the culture of variety rather than a monoculture. To make this possible it is necessary to establish the legal and financial basis for equality of opportunity, to create an inspectorate structure capable of dealing with this diversity and to guarantee freedom in teacher

training. School organization should show corresponding diversity
in its management and leadership.

Understanding of Different Educational Practices

We wish to develop tolerance and to encourage understanding
among the various educational approaches. Respect for difference
cannot flourish under the pressures of dogmas from commercial or
political interests.

The European Forum for Freedom in Education has given itself
the task of monitoring how the right to education in a free and
diverse educational structure is being practised in the different
European cultures. It intends to publish progress as well as
setbacks in the extension of such rights and to issue regular reports
for each country in Europe as a contribution to the development
in freedom in Education.

Education Act 1944

Part 4, Clause 76

In the exercise and performance of all powers and duties conferred
and imposed on them by this Act the Minister and local education
authorities shall have regard to the general principle that, in so far
as is compatible with the provision of efficient instruction and
training and the avoidance of unreasonable public expenditure,
pupils are to be educated in accordance with the wishes of their
parents.

Education Reform Bill (1988)

Lord Young of Dartington moved the following Amendment
(No.230):

After Clause 94, insert the following new clause:
("*New foundation schools.*
Extension of parental choice

(1) The Secretary of State may also enter into an agreement with any charity under which

(a) that charity undertakes to establish and maintain, and to carry on or provide for the carrying on of, an independent school to be known as a new foundation school, being a school for children at primary as well as secondary level in a rural as well as an urban area and which offers an extension of choice in respect of educational principle, in respect of size of school, in respect of curricular emphasis in addition to that on science and technology, in respect of method of teaching or which espouses a particular faith or philosophy provided the school is open, without discrimination, to all children in its catchment area; and having such further characteristics as are specified in the agreement and in subsection (2) below; and

(b) the Secretary of State agrees to make payments to that charity in consideration of those undertakings.

(2) The further characteristics mentioned above are that the school -

(a) provides education free of charge by means of an academically comprehensive intake for pupils of mixed abilities who are wholly or mainly drawn from the area in which the school is situated;

(b) admits pupils on the basis of criteria compatible with the practice of local education authorities if it cannot accept all applicants;

(c) on inspection shows that it provides an efficient education;

(d) does not propagate doctrines tending to foment racial, religious or other forms of intolerance;

(e) has a curriculum such that there are not barriers to the transfer of new foundation pupils to or from county or voluntary schools;

(f) should be funded at a unit cost per pupil not in excess of the unit costs in schools at the appropriate level maintained by the local education authority.

(3) The provision of section 94(3), (4), (5) and (6) above (which set out the conditions and requirements on which payments depend) shall also apply to new foundation schools.").

The amendment was not carried.

Education Act (1993)

Chapter IV
Establishing New Grant-Maintained Schools
Proposals for establishment of new grant-maintained schools

Section 49-(1) Where any persons (referred to in this Part of this Act as 'promoters') propose to establish a grant-maintained school, they shall -

> (a) publish proposals for that purpose in such manner as may be prescribed, and
> (b) submit a copy of the published proposals to the Secretary of State.

(2) Before publishing any proposal under this section the promoters shall consult -

> (a) the funding authority, and
> (b) such other persons as appear to be appropriate;

and in discharging their duty under this subsection, the promoters shall have regard to any guidance given from time to time by the Secretary of State.

(3) A local education authority may not establish any grant-maintained school.

(4) In relation to England this section has effect at any time after the funding authority have begun to exercise their functions.

Appendix IV

Books and Resources

Boyd W L & Kerchner C T, *The Politics of Excellence & Choice in Education*, Falmer, 1987.

Feintuck M, *Accountability & Choice in Schooling*, Open University Press, 1994.

Fernandez A & Jenkner S (Eds), *International Declarations and Conventions on the Right to Education and the Freedom of Education*, Info 3 Verlag, 1995.

Fuchs E (Ed), *Towards Freedom in Education*, Info 3 Verlag, 1993.

Gardner H, *The Unschooled Mind*, Fontana, 1995.

Hargreaves D, *The Mosaic of Learning*, Demos, 1994.

Henig J R, *Re-thinking School Choice: Limits of Market Metaphor*, Princetown, 1993.

Hodgetts C, *Inventing a School*, Resurgence, 1991.

Kelly A V, *The National Curriculum: A Critical Review*, 2nd Edition, 1995.

Jenkner S, *The Right to Education and the Freedom of Education in European Constitutions*, Info 3 Verlag, 1994.

Johnson D, *Parental Choice in Education*, Unwin Hyman, 1990.

Meighan R & Toogood P, *Anatomy of Choice in Education*, Education Now, 1992.

North R, *Schools of Tomorrow*, Green Books, 1987.

Rogers M, *Opting Out: Choice and the Future of Schools*, Lawrence & Wishart, 1992.

OECD, *School: A Matter of Choice*, 1994.

Orr D, *Earth in Mind*, Island Press, 1994.

Orr D, *Ecological Literacy*, State University of New York Press, 1992.

Seymour F, *Miracle in East Harlem: The Fight for Choice in Public Education*, Random House, 1993.

Thomson J, *Natural Childhood*, Gaia Press, 1994.

Walford G, *Choice & Equity in Education*, Cassel, 1994.

Woodhead M & McGrath A, *Family, School & Society*, Hodder & Stoughton

Video: Education on a Human Scale, Coleridge Video, 1993.

LIST OF ORGANISATIONS

Christian Schools Trust
8 Ascension Road
Romford
Essex RM5 3RS

Citizenship Foundation
Weddel House
13 West Smithfield
London EC1A 9HY

Education Now
PO Box 186
Ticknall
Derbyshire DE7 1WF

Education Otherwise
25 Common Lane
Hemingford Abbots
Cambridgeshire

European Forum for
Freedom in Education (UK)
96 Carlingcott
Near Bath BA2 8AW

European Forum for
Freedom in Education
International Office
Annener Berg 15
Witten D58454 Germany

Human Scale Education
96 Carlingcott
Nr Bath BA2 8AW

Institute for Democracy in
Education
School of Education
University of Birmingham
Birmingham B15 2TT

Irish Steiner Schools Association
Holywood Rudolf Steiner School
34 Croft Road, Holywood
Co. Down BT18 0PR
01232 428029

Muslim Schools Association
88 Sparkenhoe Street
Leicester LE2 0TA

Steiner Schools Fellowship
Michael Hall School
Forest Row, Sussex

Appendix V

The European Forum for Freedom in Education - E.F.F.E.

John Thompson

In what way and to what extent is freedom a key element in education, which after all has to serve a free democratic society? How does freedom relate to the other vital elements, such as social cohesion, fairness in access and in opportunity, and the restrictions involved in a proper distribution of the resources which enable education to happen? The intervention of the state in education (assuming its intentions are innocent) is seen as necessary to arbitrate between the claims of the different elements. Such assumed innocence hardly conceals the real interests which the state wishes to promote, and we have observed the education process becoming increasingly a matter for political decisions. These are imposed on schools, teachers and programmes to achieve a grand uniform solution to the competing claims, and also as a universal remedy to the all-too-visible ailments. The recipes for cure change with changing governments (even during a single government), as first one weakness, then another, is highlighted. There is little evidence that the choice of remedy rests on any far-reaching research into the nature of education. We see repeatedly the paradoxical situation, in that each solution is in practice only temporary and provisional, yet in theory it has for a time absolute authority, justifying its universal application.

The subjection of education to politics has led to the centralised control of curriculum and assessment procedures, to the reduction of the teachers' responsibility and to the increasing emphasis on the factual and measurable. In the UK there has been at the same time a greater autonomy in budgetary and administrative matters but, accompanied as it is by a loss of autonomy in the teaching process, it remains to be seen to what extent this represents a healthy development.

The Forum (E.F.F.E.), which was the main body to organise the Oxford Conference, aims to defend and extend school, teacher and parent autonomy. The Forum did not originate out of the British situation, but was founded in 1990 from a joint German-Hungarian initiative, following the collapse of the Communist regimes of eastern Europe. Successive conferences have shown the relevance of its aims to many other European countries, including Britain.

In the UK, the word 'freedom' in education is easily linked with A. S. Neill, or the lax and libertarian practices which are supposed to have wrecked our schools. In the European context, it argues for the reduction of state control and the assumption of greater responsibility by those immediately involved. The Forum has no narrow doctrinal approach, and the demarcation line between state and private education is seen as contingent on historical factors, and not in itself a significant factor in the evaluation of good education. It believes that all schools and teachers have the right to develop new methods, to explore new programme areas and to research new ways to serve the actual needs of each child. This freedom is inseparable from responsibility. Decrease in freedom inevitably leads to decrease in responsibility. Contemporary society relies more and more on the responsibility of its citizens. If this is not a professional part of the teachers' job, how can it become a reality for their pupils?

The Forum challenges the notion that 80% of the curriculum should be dictated by the state. It challenges the right of inspectors to impose their ethos and ideology on schools, while accepting their role as protectors of the child's rights. It is aware of the rights of minorities, and that ethnic or religious groups have legitimate claims in the education process. School movements with a distinctive educational philosophy, such as Steiner/Waldorf schools, also require acknowledgement.

The rights of parents to choose a school for their child is considered basic, and merely confirms a resolution of the European Parliament. Methods for the proper distribution of resources, so that a healthy freedom and diversity can permeate education, need to be examined. The present manipulative control is not appropriate. The implementation of a fair method of funding is a vital concern of the Forum.

The Forum is made up of members who believe that
development and renewal can only come from the strength of
individuals working together in a common aim. As they come from
the different countries of Europe, it is possible to see the strengths
and weaknesses in each national educational practice, and from
this to find new ways to solve difficulties.

The work of the Forum is centred in the conferences held
annually, and in the series of publications listed below.
Conferences have been held in various European cities, and in
May, 1996 will move to Vienna. Each conference has its
presentations by outstanding speakers, its discussions, its working
groups, as well as its open market for innovative ideas, special
approaches, etc. Working groups cover a wide range of topics.
Those on Inspection and on the Rights of Minorities have
extended over several conferences, and resulted in the production
of valuable documents.

The administration of the Forum is centred in Witten, Germany,
London and Budapest, Hungary. The patrons of the Forum are the
Presidents of Hungary and Slovenia.

Publications:

Siegfried Jenkner, *International Declarations and Conventions on the
Right to Education and the Freedom of Education.* This is now
greatly expanded in a re-issue by A Fernandez and S. Jenkner
as Vol. 8.

E Fuchs and I Krampen, *Self-Governed Schools - Case Studies,*
Info-3, Stuttgart

Appendix VI

Following up **Freeing Education**

Do you want to discuss and debate the options for freeing education in your school or organisation?

If so, speakers and resources are available to help stimulate discussion about the issues raised in this book. Please contact:

Human Scale Education, 96 Carlingcott, Nr Bath, BA2 8AW (01761 433733).

Book orders

If you have difficulty ordering from a bookshop, *Freeing Education* can also be obtained from Hawthorn Press, 1 Lansdown Lane, Stroud, Gloucestershire, GL5 1BJ
TEL (01453 757040)   FAX (01453 751138)